The Evolutionary Entrepreneur

Embarking on a New Path

Dedicated to...

The many creative entrepreneurs embarking on
new paths, which include many
challenges and rewards along the way.

May they enrich themselves and their communities
through their entrepreneurial ventures.

Mark Burwell

The Evolutionary Entrepreneur

Embarking on a New Path

Mark Burwell

Evolutions Group Publishing

ISBN-13: 978-1-7327405-0-1

Printed and bound in the U.S.A.

2019 Edition

The Evolutionary Entrepreneur
Embarking on a New Path

By Mark Burwell

Published by Evolutions Group Publishing
Cover design, editing and layout by
Cheri Larson, Larson Creative Services

This book is a collection of the author's speeches, lectures,
presentations, and editorial columns. It is sold with the understanding
that the publisher and author are not engaged in rendering any legal,
financial, or other professional services from this publication.

Evolutions Group books are available for special events or educational
purposes. For speeches, presentations and business architecting, contact
markburwell@evolutionsgroup.com. For more information, visit
www.evolutionsgroup.com

Table of Contents

FOREWORD

By Cheri Larson

As a life-long entrepreneur, I have spent over 35 years launching and operating a number of successful small businesses. From the days of lemonade stands and beaded jewelry stands on the sidewalk, any kind of business starts with a vision or dream and then the hard work begins. Research, planning, product design, marketing and then day-to-day operations are all part of the puzzle. It is never enough to "have a dream". It's how you take that dream from vision to reality to success that counts as an entrepreneur.

Over the years, I have had some great ideas that transformed into successful businesses and I have also had some not-so-great ventures. The challenges I discovered along the way never stopped me. They only gave me more knowledge for improvement and the ability to evolve as an entrepreneur. Each and every failure taught me how to "do it better next time". Each success taught me to be grateful and give back.

I grew up in an entrepreneurial family. My parents owned their own business and I watched them dream, struggle, innovate, and find success. I learned the process is never easy, but it is never dull. The ability to be in charge of your own destiny is intoxicating. Once you've worked for yourself and discovered your inner strength and ingenuity, you can never turn back.

Being an entrepreneur allows you to dream big dreams, explore the possibilities and keep striving to be better. It offers you the opportunity to share your gifts with others in many different ways. Today, I am surrounded by many friends and family who are entrepreneurs. I take delight in watching them follow their dreams and explore opportunities. In 2010, I was fortunate enough to take part in a US State Department venture pairing women entrepreneurs from the U.S. with Middle Eastern women in business. I realized through mentoring these amazing women,

I gained much more than I could possibly give. The sharing of ideas, dreams and passion is universal. Entrepreneurs share a special spirit and understand that taking a risk is all part of the territory if you want to make things happen.

One of the key turning points in my career was when I became humble enough to reach out for help. I heard about the Urban Hope Entrepreneur Center from a friend and even though I had been in business for years, I decided to check out what they had to offer. That's when I met Mark Burwell, a mentor who would eventually become my husband 15 years later.

I quickly discovered that I didn't *know it all*. The most important thing I discovered was the peer-to-peer guidance and connections I gained would enable me to grow in ways that I never could have imagined.

The people I met through the Entrepreneur Center all those years ago have remained my strongest mentors and business allies to this day. The things I learned and the people I met by reaching out changed the trajectory of my business and my life.

I was lucky enough years ago to be put on a path with incredible mentors, like Mark Burwell and many others in the Urban Hope/E-Hub program. In this book, Mark offers practical advice, garnered from years of working with and mentoring thousands of entrepreneurs in many areas. His advice is solid, inspirational and most of all easy-to-implement. I hope that you learn from his sage wisdom and find the people to empower you and help you evolve as an entrepreneur of influence. One of my favorite quotes is by Eleanor Roosevelt and it has truly been my mantra throughout the years of entrepreneurship and life in general . . . ***"You must do the thing you think you cannot do."***

I invite you to embark on your entrepreneurial path today and never look back!

The Evolutionary Entrepreneur

Mark Burwell plays cupid minus the cutesy wings and without the showy bow and arrow. He coined the word cupiding© to describe his brand of networking and it squarely hits the target.

Mark is uniquely qualified as an evolutionary entrepreneur himself after successful tenures as president and CEO, growing a successful Midwest menswear retail and catalog business. He founded a *light years ahead of its time* retail and corporate gourmet foods, coffee and gift business. As chief business architect of his own consulting business, he has put together a mentorship-in-residence program.

He has also revolutionized a non-profit entrepreneur center into a model for building communities. The Urban Hope Entrepreneur Center, know as "E-Hub" has connected budding entrepreneurs with peer-to-peer connections to give them start-up wings.

The award-winning advocate, mentor, author and speaker, shares his collection of speeches, talks, and columns in his book series "The Evolutionary Entrepreneur".

With his "energy in overdrive" personality, the former collegiate standout track sprinter says, "entrepreneurship is not a spectator sport". He is embarking on a new path with his partner Cheri Larson, co-authoring a new book, "Growing Your Creative Business" and hosting workshops for creativepreneurs around the US and internationally.

Article published in Green Bay Area Chamber of Commerce's Bay Business Journal, *"Green Bay's Fabulous 50 You Should Know"*.

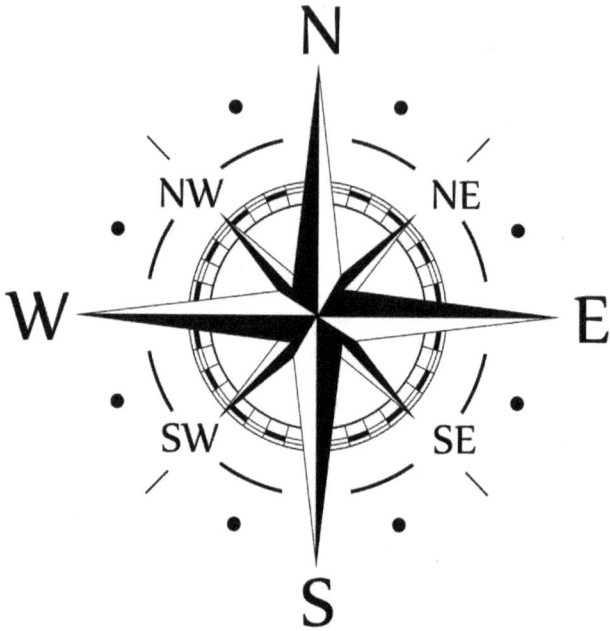

"Your passion is your internal compass that will guide you from where you are towards where you want to go."

- Julie Conner

CHAPTER 1

Embarking on a New Path

It's true that in the new entrepreneurs journey, as in life, great opportunities, challenges and discoveries wait around every turn. The business that thrives is usually the business that dips its toe in the water to test the temperature, but then does a search ahead to get a glimpse of a better tomorrow. That entrepreneur celebrates the spirit of innovative thinking and curiosity in the same spirit that allows businesses to be champions and leaders in our communities.

Why are we frightened of new ideas when we should be frightened of old ones? As we go on our journey, we must learn how to escape old concepts.

"We must continually evolve and reinvent ourselves, especially in the world of marketing and technology, which has the shelf life of fruit."

Following the path of least resistance sometimes brings failures in life. Once you have crossed the line on the path to success, start a new race, to keep you, your employees and customers ahead. Believe that the best is yet to come in your journey. This is the passion of being a true entrepreneur.

Create the future rather than fear it. Security is less about the negative economy and more about what you have learned. History and statistics are not something we read about, but something we make.

Our communities congratulate and embrace you.

"Be not the slave of your own past – plunge into the sublime seas, dive deep and swim far, so you shall come back with self-respect, with new power, with an advanced experience that shall explain and overlook the old."

- Emerson

CHAPTER 2

Evolving into New Frontiers

We are evolving into new frontiers with an overabundance of math, science, technology and industrialization. This has created a stress on the left-brain and analytical mind. This is the road to today. The evolutionary entrepreneur will bring creativity, innovation, wisdom and social enterprising to our journey to tomorrow.

To evolve into the new frontiers, you need to take some detours at times. You must always be evolving. New innovation and ideas can be revolutionary, but evolution is essential to long-term success.

As the tide broadens, the waves may become higher and more demanding. Have your boat ready. Believe in hope and do not fear.

Being an evolutionary entrepreneur means you will need to contribute a value proposition to your business, clients, customer, community, and beyond. This value proposition is an asset and give you need to identify. It will be the energy that drives you.

To become an evolutionary entrepreneur you need to pursue the opportunity, even with limited resources. Your resources to start may only be a vision, some concepts and an opportunity in the marketplace. But as we know, the old ideas and businesses fade away. Your opportunity may be to fill this vacuum, with a new concept idea or value.

Yes, inventors and entrepreneurs are disruptors and modern day revolutionary entrepreneurs. I continue to see and work with many dreamers who have evolved their concepts into the marketplace and have become small giants. They may not be the

Steve Jobs, Henry Fords, or Bill Gates, but they are redefining niches in the marketplace.

I also like to think of an evolutionary entrepreneur as someone who creates freedom in his or her lifestyle. In today's world, you can work anywhere in the world. As an evolutionary entrepreneur, you can create the flexibility to follow your passion and dreams on your journey to tomorrow.

"We cannot tell what may happen to us in the strange medley of life. But we can decide what happens in us, how we take it, what we do with it, and that is what really counts in the end."

-Joseph Fort Newton

CHAPTER 3

A Recipe for Success

The hallmark of an entrepreneur is embarking on new paths with the desire to evolve and improve. Strong entrepreneurs know they cannot be all things to all people. Most of them have one thing in common, and that is to use their unique perspective.

These entrepreneurs share a number of attributes that are needed for an entrepreneur's success along their journey.

The first is **Vision.** Your enterprise team, family and employees must share this vision.

Empowerment and **Confidence** are vital. Failure is not in your vocabulary. Negotiating skills are important.

Commitment is your engagement to devotion and passion.

Priorities and Timing is important.

Hitting the target means you must be **Results Oriented.**

Perseverance is persistence and determination in overcoming the obstacles along your path.

Innovation is crucial. You need to evolve and reinvent which means sometimes going outside your comfort zone.

Intuition. Good entrepreneurs and leaders need to follow their gut instinct to make good and timely decisions.

Lastly, **a Sense of Giving Back.** Great entrepreneurs believe in not just growing their businesses, but also their communities.

In the final analysis, entrepreneurship is a new path of discovery, freedom and empowerment.

"The stars will never align, and the traffic lights of life will never all be green at the same time. The universe doesn't conspire against you, but it doesn't go out of its way to line up the pins either. Conditions are never perfect. 'Someday' is a disease that will take your dreams to the grave with you. Pro and con lists are just as bad. If it's important to you and you want to do it 'eventually,' just do it and correct course along the way."

- Tim Ferriss

CHAPTER 4

Taking Your Victory Lap

My last three books, *Stepping Up to New Opportunities, Beyond the Passion* and *The Path to Today...The Journey to Tomorrow,* were written to spark discussion and evolutionary thinking for entrepreneurs. Many of these concepts are incorporated throughout this book.

While evolving is change during our time on this planet, being an entrepreneur we all are chasing our vision and mission in life. So when we finish the race we have to strive to win.

Winning and being successful means a lot of hard work and sacrifice. But there comes a time when we embark on retirement, which I like to refer to it as reclaiming your fire by taking a *Victory Lap.*

Baby boomers are moving into their retirement years. I have connected with many and I stress to them not to get into saying the "retirement" word. If this describes you, try reconnecting with your mission or community.

I have been blessed with two successful sons, Shawn and Ryan, who graduated from the University of Wisconsin system and Marquette University. They have continued their careers with Wisconsin-based family owned Fortune 500 companies. Along with their wives Angie and Cindy, they are embarking on new paths while raising their children, Eleanor, Gus, Aubriana and Gwyneth. Cheri and I, along with her children Katie, Annika and Robb have created an extended family as we start this next chapter of our lives.

We are continuing on a new path of cultural immersion as we travel around the world meeting many creative entrepreneurs.

Many times in our lives we don't have time to truly engage in giving back because of our work or parenting. But now is the time! *The future needs you!*

As we go into retirement we need to take our *Victory Lap*. So take a deep breath and return home as Dorothy discovered in the Wizard of Oz...your heart is your ticket home. We need to remind ourselves of the precious time we have left on earth. This new path, returning to a place called home, may be volunteering to make the community a better place for the younger generation. Maybe it will be mentoring, caregiving, or offering to help with the underserved.

We need to take this path to visit friends and family, business associates and even customers. Don't perceive that your climb is over. Yes, you have gone through the finish line by retiring, but enjoy the simple things as well. It may be golfing, travel or reading that book to your grandkids.

Many who are divorced or widowed will realize that the final lap is about building relationships all over. It is about giving and receiving, caring and being cared for, loving and being loved.

Strong communities exist because we recognize the needs. Businesses find their market and place goods and services where needed. Educators and our public service make our community safer and efficient. Non-profit charities fill in where there is a need to help. So we need to be makers and givers to continue to have a strong community.

As I climbed the path to the Bell Rock in Sedona, Arizona, pictured on the front cover of this book, the energy of the surroundings reminded me that there are still many new paths to embark upon, even after retirement.

CHAPTER 5

Make Sure You Have Your Compass Before Starting the Journey

As the years have gone by, I have worked less with launching start-up businesses but increased working with growth businesses. They are providing great opportunity for economic development with capital improvements to their businesses and providing more jobs. The successful ones I have encouraged to navigate change and always be evolving.

We are in a world of evolution. It is accelerating faster and faster. Using some of the concepts in practice from my book and workshops, *The Evolutionary Entrepreneur...the Path to Today, the Journey to Tomorrow,* has provided a compass to help entrepreneurs navigate the rough waters in the economic environment.

A few points in learning to survive include:
- Yes, you need to go outside your comfort zone. For baby boomers this means keeping pace with technology, both internally and externally. Some technology may have to be outsourced. You don't need to know everything!

- Learn how to recover quickly and adapt to mistakes. Try this by taking smaller risks outside your comfort zone so you can recover.

- As entrepreneurs, stretch your day but incorporate social time, family time, pace yourself with personal time and of course wellness and fitness time. Everything doesn't have to be jammed into the 9 to 5 time period.

- Learn to position your business to be sustainable forever or to transition to sell.

- Treat every staff in your company as a business partner not just as an employee. Learn to mentor and empower them.

- Broaden your partnerships and resources. Learn how to make productive connections. Stay away from the *energy and negative vampires.*

- Build and use both the creative and analytical sides of your brain to develop the skills needed. Exercise builds the body emotionally and constant learning is oxygen to the brain and it thrives on it.

- Don't procrastinate. I find that busy entrepreneurs tend to procrastinate on the little and easy things and avoid tackling the big projects. You need to learn how to take baby steps and stay on task.

- Learn how to be flexible. This can be the hardest part of developing change. Seasons change, the sun and moon change, and you need to evolve as well.

- Lastly, so you don't develop burnout, be resilient. Have a positive attitude and be proactive to change and challenges. Set time for opportunities to play. Don't be a martyr.

CHAPTER 6

Decide Your Destiny . . . Dare to Dream

Dreams are important because we use our imagination. As I help with the dreams of entrepreneurs, I want them to use their innovative ability. But fuel is needed in this imagination to make your dreams become a reality.

Everything starts with our passions and thoughts. Helping craft the visions of entrepreneurs is to justify their new lifestyle and set their values to relate back into helping build their communities as well. This helps them achieve their success.

"One dream, one idea can change the world. Dare to dream . . . seize your idea."

You can't do everything yourself. Family, friends, advisors, peers, business partners and resources are all needed. Create a creative environment around you so you all see through the same lens. Keep them on a steady diet of motivation. Fresh stimuli are a key element to success.

Dare to step out boldly. Don't be afraid to be disruptive on your new product, services or concept. Dream to see the many opportunities for you and the customers.

In one of the chapters in my recent book I talk about the right and left sides of our brain. Let's not forget that our psyche is made up of both masculine (power) and feminine (capacity to love) attributes.

In order to have good entrepreneurial success we need to be the boat and also the dock. The boat is the business, which has a lot of waves, but we must be grounded to the dock, which includes our family, peers and friends.

When you dare to dream, you must have the courage to work hard to achieve your goals. You need to wake up and face the real world to plan and map out your vision.

Dreaming, simply put is *hope,* which gives us the courage to attain our vision. Let yourself decide your destiny. Dreams enable us to build our existence in this world.

"Good dreams expand our hearts

and enlighten our minds.

Dreams need to become a great meal.

They must taste good, smell good,

but be nutritious in the long run."

CHAPTER 7

Reclaiming the Fire

A growing number of 50+ adults are turning into solo entrepreneurs. We call them **Encore Entrepreneurs.** This select group of individuals is creating new lifestyle changes. Are you close to retirement and exploring new opportunities? Do you have a plan for managing your life after you retire? Encore Entrepreneurs are not just creating jobs but meeting community needs and finding their passion later in life.

Civic Ventures, a think tank on boomers reports that aspiring entrepreneurs have an average of over 30 years of work experience and 12 years of community service. Five out of six have management experience.

A recent study by the Kaufmann Foundation found that Americans aged 55 to 64 are starting up new business ventures at a higher rate than any other age group. Some are now financially secure. Others have been dislocated from the workforce by the recession and feel this is a better option to give them more flexibility for their lifestyle.

For many boomers, 50's are now the new 20's and 30's.

"As your life changes, it takes time to recalibrate, to find your values again. You might also find that retirement is the time when you stretch out and find your potential."
- Sid Miramontes

13

""If you can't fly then run. If you can't run, then walk. And, if you can't walk, then crawl, but whatever you do, you have to keep moving forward."

- Martin Luther King, Jr.

CHAPTER 8

Boomer Entrepreneurs

Studies have shown that 3 out of 4 Americans over 50 want to look at working into there sixties and beyond. One of the chapters in my recent book talks about *Encore Entrepreneurs.* Because of major downsizing, job burnout and forced retirements, more boomers are looking at entrepreneurship as an opportunity to create their footprint in life or earn extra income. Many I have talked to say they have gotten an advanced degree or certifications only to be passed over due to their age.

Shift Happens...culture and technology change, but putting that gray hair to use via volunteering or entrepreneurship keeps the experience, skills sets, mentoring and wisdom in our American economy, giving us the edge in the global competition.

I want to speak from my own experience of 6 years in the corporate world, 22 years of starting, owning and running a handful of award winning companies and topping off 17 years of growing and modeling a successful non-profit entrepreneur program. After 45 years I did retire from a full time position. It was important to me to continue to volunteer on various boards, give back by working with community and businesses leaders, teach at various colleges, write books and speak professionally.

Remember to always continue to be a person of influence. Age doesn't matter. Stay young by giving back, leaving a footprint or pursue the passion or hobby you always wanted to explore. Today, you can work from almost anywhere. I like to head for warmer climate to escape cold Wisconsin winters or weave my travel with work, but at my own pace.

Some tips and questions to consider for **Boomer Entrepreneurs:**
- Will you enjoy your new endeavor?
- Is there a market for your service or product?

- Don't wing it! Take an entrepreneur training series and not just a quick workshop. One that includes getting a business plan.
- Do you have some additional cash to launch a micro-enterprise?
- Try to be an independent solo-entrepreneur.
- Don't get involved with a business that is a risk. It is like your investment strategy – you diversify and avoid risk.
- Don't get trapped into a franchise. This is a long-term strategy and full-time commitment.
- Make sure you can interact with people, especially if you are alone.
- Perhaps a location at home or one that allows a pet.
- Understand your physical limitations and energy.

Lastly, remember as a kid when you always wanted to have a little spending money? You may have babysat, mowed lawns or had a lemonade stand. Now it's time to craft your **Boomer Entrepreneur** concept. Throw some money into your piggy bank, explore the opportunities, enjoy your accomplishments, and feel young as a kid again.

The price of success has been hard work, commitment to the job and a determination to get through some tough times.

To accomplish great things and be the best we must not only act, but also dream…not only plan, but also believe. Our most painful moments will come when we must admit we were not prepared.

The secret of our success is to be ready when opportunity comes. Then, when we have done our best, given our all and in the process supplied the needs of our families and our society, we will know we have succeeded.

CHAPTER 9

Reflections on the Path Ahead

As I reflect on the past, I wanted to share some things on the entrepreneurial outlook. I look forward to having the opportunity to talk about several of these points with my talks, workshops and recent book across the country and abroad. I look forward to travel and cultural immersion with my talented wife Cheri who is also a life-long entrepreneur. We hope to enjoy time and engage with many exciting creative entrepreneurs around the world.

Here are some of the key points of discussion I will share:
- We need to build a stronger and entrepreneurial ecosystem. That means making all the connections come together which was our vision for E-Hub in becoming a hub to connect and foster entrepreneurship.
- Entrepreneurs are the strength of todays US Economy. Small and micro-business is what creates jobs both skilled and unskilled to help our main streets, urban and rural areas.

- Crowd funding, venture capital and other forms of funding equity have blossomed and help many entrepreneurs.

- Start-ups have slowed but that's okay because we need to grow second stage businesses into what I call the Parent Stage. More business modeling is needed and more custom workshops.

- We must help our lawmakers and policymakers to understand! Many have never been in small business and do not understand how to build a level playing field for small business.

- Review our taxes and investments.

- Teach and foster the young to get engaged. Have our school systems teach that free enterprise is not a bad thing. Tap into their creativity.

- Have the communities learn to give back – not the entrepreneurs only – government education and community leaders need to make commitments to the ecosystem.

- Include all the awesome artisans! They create a community of value.

- Cultivate our champions of innovation.

"Ideas are easy.

Implementation is hard."

- Guy Kawasaki

CHAPTER 10

Football and Business:
Finding the Winning Combination

The football season is very important in Wisconsin, whether it be the Green Bay Packers, Wisconsin Badgers or the many high school teams. Many times I look at running a football team the same as running an enterprise because you need a lot of the same attributes.

Years ago, I was fortunate to share these traits with former Green Bay Packers coach, player and NFL Hall of Famer Forest Gregg. I've also had the same discussions while enjoying dinner with Green Bay Packers legendary NFL Hall of Famer Willie Davis. I have a signed picture of both of them in their game uniform hanging above my desk as a reminder of their leadership as Coach Lombardi's co-captains. Years later as I spoke to them off the field I saw why they were leaders.

Based on their experiences as well as conversations with other players including Fuzzy Thurston, Ray Nitschke, Dave Robinson and the legendary Reggie White, I have had the opportunity to share with entrepreneurs how they need to have leaders on the field like a football team. Listed below are some of those traits that I used in the success of growing my business:

- **You need a quarterback.** Someone who can run your offense. They need to get the respect of the team or staff. Find someone you can delegate to.

- **Pick out leaders and mentors** who will lead by example. Leaders who can motivate others and develop a culture of a winning attitude.

- **Know your competition.** As an entrepreneur, don't you need to know the down and distance? Don't they also

19

need to get into the film room each week? Entrepreneurs need to focus on details of the marketplace, customers and their cash flow.

- **Be aware of the clock.** Time management is really important on the field. Entrepreneurs also have only 24/7/365. I stress to entrepreneurs to be innovative in their tasks. Try to shed the *energy vampires*. Reggie White shaped the Super Bowl team by challenging the players, especially the non-performers.

- **Preparation.** Study the playbook, then practice, practice and workout. As the owner or leader of the enterprise you need to execute the top priorities.

- **Involvement in the community.** Working with Lombardi Legends like Fuzzy Thurston, Ray Nitschke and their wives, allowed me to give back. Their non-profits were important to the community. Giving back is the key to building a strong community. It's one of the most important things I stress with entrepreneurs as they become empowered as mentors and community leaders.

- **Trust your decision-making.** This is all about confidence.

- **Lastly, passion and commitment is key.**

"In life, as in football, you won't go far unless you know where the goalposts are"
-Arnold H. Glasgow

20

CHAPTER 11

Time Out!

Entrepreneurs are on the playing field all the time because they feel they will get behind or miss an opportunity. But, there are times to call "Time Out!"

You need to assess your past year or season. Be honest and look yourself in the mirror. You need to truly know where you are at financially and positioned within your market and what your environment is within your industry sector.

Next, is your operation up with the times? Are your employees walking in sand at times? Do a walk through and assess your position as well as everyone's on efficiency and time. Don't let your tools, procedures or technology bog you or your team down.

Always be looking for opportunities and innovations. Evolve and always be reinventing yourself.

Do not forget to evaluate your customer list. Who are your best and are you paying enough attention to them or taking them for granted. Even though they may be spenders they need attention.

Fire your suspects! I'm talking about the wheelers and dealers, the complainers and late payers.

Take the stress out of your life and empower yourself.

Learn to say no to energy vampires. Do a time study on everyone, including yourself. Who are the time wasters?

Uncage yourself from emails and social media. Be positive and not negative. Sometimes employees, partners, customers, suppliers, family or even friends have the doom and gloom attitude – shake it!

Who truly is your competition? Is it in the same product or service field? It may be money spent to satisfy the marketplace outside your exact niche, but a dollar spent is a dollar spent.

Who are your partners? Do they need more attention as well? Are they mentors, resources, or part of your business solution?

Are your business-related outside activities wasting your time, money or energy?

Lastly, how does everyone see you? Evaluate your image, brand, community and market influence.

Step back and call a time out, which isn't always just a vacation but a chance to regroup.

"Always dream and shoot higher than you know you can do. Don't bother just to be better than your contemporaries or predecessors. Try to be better than yourself."

- William Faulkner

CHAPTER 12

Building a Community of Entrepreneurs

Innovative communities are vibrant when they are creative in nurturing entrepreneurship, accepting diversity, new lifestyles and culture.

New ideas and change are the growth engines of tomorrow. Opportunities will reside in a community that empower people with the ability to express innovation.

Some communities are conservative. They do not reward change or innovation and are dying as a result.

- We must pay attention and create an entrepreneurial eco-system. This should include a vibrant downtown with culture, nightlife, music, commerce, restaurants, artists, entrepreneurs, affordable leases and spaces, churches, and new neighborhoods
- We must pass the ball as a team. Organizations must become connectors and collaborate to get everyone into the game.
- We must challenge conventional wisdom and tap into young creative talent and energy.
- We must convert the negatives into the positives. Dare to be different. Do not look back at what should have been done.
- Remove mediocrity of programs, rural sprawl, bad entitlements, schools, and social and environmental degradation.

Take responsibility for this change. Make things happen!

What is important to Entrepreneurs?
Entrepreneurs need a level playing field that includes:

23

- Non-intimidating government – Less negativity and more positive encouragement.
- Access to talent – Knowledge and trainable workers.
- Access to capital – Innovative-seed capital. Need more start-up financing.
- Networking opportunities – Cupiding© is the strength of the E-Hub's peer-to-peer mentoring concept. We teach and foster how to develop:
    - Strategic alliance partners
    - Service providers
    - Resources, government
- Infrastructure - Local institutional and government support. High-speed internet access, creative and fair developers, safe streets, etc.

What can we do?
We need to foster and nurture the eco-system.

Public officials, businesses, and citizens alike need to give recognition. It requires a mix of good programs, a good quality of life, and a culture that encourages people to take risks and start new ventures. If this is established, the benefits are great.

Bad public policy can cripple entrepreneurship. If the price of failure is too high, commerce and economic activity will become fizzled. Resources must become more accessible.

We need to be a participant not a spectator. Community leaders cannot guarantee success or prevent failure. However, it is their responsibility to provide the encouragement, necessary tools and knowledge to succeed.

"There are some things we cannot learn from others. You have to pass through the fire."
- Norman Douglas

CHAPTER 13

The Rise of Creativepreneurs

What is a *Creativepreneur*? There are many vocations that a creative individual may follow, including photography, web design, restaurateur, digital marketing, home staging, interior design, hair styling, urban farming, health coaching, event planning, floral design . . . the list is endless. What makes these people unique is their passion for creativity and usually, their disinterest or fear in the aspects of running a business.

To succeed as a creativepreneur, you need to develop not only your talents, but your ability to bring them to the world in the most effective way. Creativepreneurs need to step outside their comfort zone and assemble their toolbox – they need to do the research, get the training, build their enterprise team and build their brand. It takes a lot of hard work, but mostly it takes a leap of faith, knowing that there are others out there to help you find your path and help you succeed.

Creatives provide our communities with a vibrant heart and soul. Businesses know that quality of life is of utmost importance in recruiting qualified talent. One of the top factors people look for is a vibrant arts and creative community.

"Build cities of creative! It's good for our economy – it's good for our souls."

We must never forget the impact the arts have in improving our communities. The arts have a long history of bringing people together across boundaries. Art serves to enrich the physical, economic, social and cultural elements of a community.
How do we empower and train creative entrepreneurs? By giving them the tools and resources needed to build a business mindset. Communities and non-profits are the beneficiaries of a strong creative community. By supporting our creatives, we all win!

"Every human has four endowments; self awareness, conscience, independent will and creative imagination. These give us the ultimate human freedom - the power to choose, to respond, to change."

- Stephen Covey

CHAPTER 14

Stay Lean to Lead the Competition

Entrepreneurs must follow the simple tip to be aware of competition, *not afraid of it*. To stay lean you must focus on the customer and not waste so much time, energy, money and sleepless nights on the competition.

Don't ignore your competition. Being aware of them means staying on top of your industry and product and service offering, and always evolving to a better level and relationship with your customers. Evolve your brand and open up your customer relationship with your clients.

When building a lean marketing approach look at your customer base in these sectors:

Suspects – Customers who are not loyal or rarely care about your brand.

Convenience – Customers who buy out of convenience or common habit.

Passive – Infrequent buyer

Referral – The loyal client who purchases. Share their loyalty and refer to others.

You must be patient in building up to the referral customer but they are your reputation and help build your profits, assets, customer-base and truly become a stakeholder in your business. My word **cupiding**[©] (coined word I use in my workshops, articles and books) also needs to be part of building this loyalty. It serves as a strong relationship but must be earned and have a good matchmaker.

In short, if you are looking for that marriage or strong relationship with your customer it must include a strong dating process including:

- Build strong, attractive websites, friendly social media to start to build the trust, then create a strong shopping or service oriented environment and experience.

- To stay lean you need to streamline and nano-target. Stay relevant.

- Finally, let the customer feel they have some control on feedback to build word-of-mouth reputation.

- Let them become your advocates. This is not done with cheap prices and low quality products or services.

This success will let you become a *customer driven company.*

"Competition is always a good thing.

It forces us to do our best.

A monopoly renders people

complacent and satisfied with

mediocrity."

-Nancy Pearcy

CHAPTER 15

Can You Understand Me Now?

What's your style? Do you ramble, lecture, tell stories, or go into a pitch? Every activity in our lives is served better with effective communications, whether you are speaking or writing. When we are unable to effectively communicate what we mean or become nervous or defensive, our message becomes diluted or blocked.

Entrepreneurs depend on effective social, personal and business communications. Great communication not only helps to build your confidence but also enables you to become a person of influence. You may have the opportunity to speak at any turn from pitching your product or service to conducting a meeting to accepting an award or persuading others to see your point of view. There are endless opportunities for speaking and it can be tortuous if you don't feel confident in your ability to communicate.

Fear of public speaking is an obstacle that can be conquered, simply by taking small steps. Here are some of my personal tips from coaching, one-on-one training and speaking to large audiences.

- Tackle specific issues – don't ramble without purpose.
- Learn to structure key points, stats and details in 24 words or less.
- Put a "wow" statement or question first. (Personally, I will always bring out the punch line first.)
- Remember, you are not telling a joke. You need to hit the main point right away.
- Never complain or become negative, especially at the start.
- Learn to prototype your ideas or sketch visually in your notes or outline.
- Demonstrate with props or exhibits.
- Use storytelling to describe situations or incidents.
- Don't memorize your talk – refer back to storytelling.
- Stay relevant to the audience.

- Don't perform **Death by PowerPoint** by reading from slides. Have confidence and don't rely on what your audience can already read.
- Practice, practice, practice impromptu remarks and be prepared for off-the-cuff situations.
- Keep it short. Rambling and going off tangent usually means you are not prepared.

Simply put, when speaking, less is better.

"The best speeches come from the heart and reflect your passion. Speak as if your life depended on it."

- Arvee Robinson

CHAPTER 16

Stop Networking and Start Connecting!

Where would we be without our contacts? Wipe out our smart phone, desktop, laptop, notebook or even our little black book and we are lost. But, are your contacts good connections?

The one who establishes the best contacts and not collecting the most business cards *wins!*

A connection is someone you know and can trust. Someone you have taken time to establish credibility with. It should not be about an immediate sale or gain, but rather, to focus on what you can do for the other person or their business. We stress in our peer-to-peer mentoring to "give back." This cannot be stressed enough. It will set you apart as a leader of influence. In other words, you need to give them something of value first, before you take or ask for something.

These points will lead you into turning your contacts into connections:
- Find your commonality
- Make sure you show them how you are going to meet their needs
- Find matching passion
- Create the demand for your product or service
- Communicate your needs as well
- Do what you promise and follow-up

In many of my past talks, image and the first impression especially the way you dress was important, and it still is! I like to ask the audience, "Do you have a smile?" If you look in the mirror before you leave each day what do you see? Successful connectors understand this concept. Take pride in yourself. Don't apologize for looking nice! Peer pressure on dressing down is an obstacle in making good connections.

Next, people want to know your reputation. What is your personal brand: Is it your dress? Webpage? Business cards? Community involvement? Personality? Or your 90 second pitch?

In summary, connecting is all about your ability to:
- Successfully engage
- Communicate your value proposition
- Learn how to become an entrepreneur of influence

"To be successful, you have to be able to relate to people. They have to be satisfied with your personality to be able to do business with you and to build a relationship with mutual trust."

- George Ross

CHAPTER 17

Flexible Workplaces and Schedules Is a Win-Win!

Entrepreneurs that are innovative in their business now need to be innovative with their best resource, *their people!*

When I was growing a statewide business as an entrepreneur, I needed to find special people and not just average people. Don't get caught into building a cookie cutter or matrix schedule to throw them in. I let the managers provide flexible hours, conditions, and benefits. With lifestyle changes, family working situations, and customer and seasonal needs it can be a win-win to make it work. Happy employees and happy families equal happy customers and happy company.

Sometimes seasonal, part-time or remote staff can be a win-win situation which I found out with Erin Kopitzke, who joined me as Program Coordinator in the early years of Urban Hope Entrepreneur Center/E-Hub as a new college graduate. She worked full time for eight months and joined her husband Casey for the remainder of the year while he played and coached for the Chicago Cubs. She also worked part time after she had her son Sam. Currently, Erin works remotely from St. Paul, Minnesota. Over the past 17 years, workplace flexibility has truly been a win-win for both of us.

The workforce is competitive, very diverse and has a multi-generational profile. Most people are time starved even with all the apps. People are better multi-taskers but entrepreneur owners and managers need to loosen the reins on freedom. Because of smartphones, laptops, document sharing, the cloud, and other tools, we need to untether the physical environment for many job duties. To enable an employee to save time and the stress of a daily commute means a lot. Flexibility even one day a week can go a long way.

This of course will not work unless you are an entrepreneurial leader who can set goals for flexible hours to keep employees flexible, productive and innovative. Performance and communication must be reviewed. I have found that trust is eventually established. Full-time hours are not always needed by employees or employers.

The government has damaged our workforce by creating a penalty for people who do want those extra hours needed for families or even single moms, because they lose benefits and should be rewarded and not penalized.

Entrepreneurs need to create positions of trust and even proud titles and responsible job duties. This helps their children see their parents as good role models, even while working at home.

I have been asked what is the best model? I say there is not a "one size fits all" answer. You are an entrepreneur. Come up with a new concept that works with flextime. Ask for proposals from staff and then evaluate and take action or test them. Then rework if they need improvement. Sharing and cross training are important to making this work.

I have found in certain positions that if the special person who you have trained and mentored is a key component and now moves away, you can continue to maintain a partial position to keep the internal spirit, expertise and productivity in place.

So consider as micro-businesses that you have the ability to be innovative and have loyal employees for a long time.

CHAPTER 18

Becoming an Entrepreneurial Hub

To be a successful business or organization you must form solid connections. I refer to the formation of these effective connections as cupiding©. These connections serve as the cornerstones that allow you to build successful business networks.

For a number of years the organization for which I was National Director was referred to Urban Hope Entrepreneur Center. After a number of years we changed it to E-Hub (Entrepreneurial Hub of Urban Hope Businesses) to better reflect our mission, which was to become the center of a constellation that includes thousands of alumni businesses, community leaders, media partners, colleges, chambers and financial lenders.

By becoming a hub business, your organization becomes a key link within a network of referrals and diverse contacts.

Points to Consider:
- Start spending time with the right connectors in quality professional environments.
- Join diverse networking groups that fit your business and its vision. Consider the basic mission and philosophy of the group, the potential for building solid relationships and the reputation of the group.
- Be conscious of how much time you can devote.
- Lastly, become a *hub* yourself. Even if you don't commit to joining a group, build your own passively.

The passive network I have established includes thousands of contacts, many which have become loyal relationships. Sometimes even casual contacts have a way of evolving into strong contacts. As hub spheres get established, these connectors become your sphere of influence, helping you to grow your business.

"Negotiation is about knowing what you want, going after it, and respecting the other person in the process. Remember that the whole point of negotiating is compromise. This means that you need to look out for yourself, but also be willing to budge in order to satisfy both parties. "

CHAPTER 19

Negotiating For a Common Goal

Negotiating is about choices. It is about the best alternatives. Entrepreneurs need a toolbox of skills when it comes to negotiating. The best way for this to happen is through preparation and understanding good business ethics.

Toolbox of Tips for Negotiating:
- Each party is looking to benefit. We must learn how to solve problems, ease tensions and build consensus.
- Never have a "take it or leave it" attitude. Be able to walk away or say, "Let's work this out."
- Learn how to create the demand.
- Timelines are important. Always include a follow-up date and an expiration date. Procrastination will spoil a lot of deals.
- Ask revealing questions to see the playing field. Who are the stakeholders?
- Learn a much as you can about your prospects.
- Develop confidence by practicing. Prepare for questions you do not want to answer.
- Do not be demanding. Be positive.
- When negotiating, people accept good news in bunches and bad news all at once.
- Frame things into opportunities.
- Always have an escape clause.

More Tips:
- Have them make the first offer.
- Never make an offer without having some concessions in your back pocket. These are your deal points.
- Stress the features and benefits.
- Negotiate on your strengths.
- Lean on your advisors and key staff when expertise is needed.

- Show patience.
- Do not major in the minors – focus on the real challenges rather than the small stuff.
- Avoid threats.
- Do not use manipulative tactics.
- Listen!

Why Things Fail:
- Overconfidence or lack of confidence.
- Not looking to give and take.
- Not understanding the marketplace or barriers.
- Not understanding the limits for both sides.

Lastly, customer service is all about negotiating as well. Establish a clear route of communication. Empower your staff to handle and negotiate challenges and complaints. Your image and reputation are at stake.

"Let us never negotiate out of fear.

But let us never fear to negotiate."

\- John F. Kennedy

CHAPTER 20

Building a Strong Enterprise Team

Designing an effective advisory team is a very important step for a small business entrepreneur, and is especially true for family businesses.

I encourage entrepreneurs and businesses to have a paid team of professional advisors such as those shown in this chapter. In addition, I recommend they add a dose of task-driven, unpaid ad hoc members who can be part of their organization's management structure.

An advisory team is not a board of directors, which serves as a fiduciary and legal authority. They do not have to make decisions or have any obligations or a sense of liability in the decision making process.

Tips on Forming an Effective Enterprise Team

The Ideal Number - To have an ad hoc committee, three seems to be an ideal number. Remember that the more you have at a meeting the less productive you will be. Each person becomes a geometric increase in trying to get a decision made.

Who to Avoid - Avoid using close friends or family. They may become too emotional to make the right business decisions.

How to Recruit - Make sure they have solid business ethics. Your business plan or your executive summary is important. Recruit people who are attracted to your business. Don't recruit professional business people for free advice.

Compensation - Reciprocating the favor as an advisor is good. Giving gift certificates from one of your clients or customers is also a good motivational tool. Don't take for granted professional advice on a pro-bono basis. Be sure to analyze and justify the payment schedule of all your paid advisors. Don't get caught in giving cash. It is never appreciated in the long run.

Meetings - Use your advisory team as a focus group and to establish strategic planning. Do not format like a bureaucratic large organization or business. This will make it easy for you to discuss your challenges and successes within your business. An agenda is still important with a time limit. Meeting two to four times a year is usually workable and acceptable for most business advisors. Don't over utilize or burn them out. Remember, they are not running your business, they are only advisors.

The key is to *listen* to your advisory team and be the decision maker. If you don't take the time to utilize any of their advice you are doing an injustice to your business.

Key Members of an Enterprise Team

- **Business Advisors** - Seek out other successful business leaders that can act as an advisor or participate on your advisory board.
- **Accountant** - Should be used for taxes and complex cash flow analysis. If you're not able to perform basic day-to-day bookkeeping, have it done by a professional.
- **Attorney** - Used for small business issues and setting up your organizational structure.
- **Insurance Agent** - Insurance is more complicated than it may appear. Make sure your agent is knowledgeable about small business and compassionate about your concerns.
- **Banker** - Interview several, feel the handshake and think of them as taking ownership in your business. Look for commitment & flexibility.
- **Technical Support** - If you are not computer savvy, you need professionals to help you understand the basics of computer software and hardware, e-commerce and technical support issues.

- **Marketing and Social Media** - You need creative people - marketing specialists, graphic designers, social media experts and others.
- **Human Resources** - Before hiring employees, make sure you have consulted with someone with employment, tax and benefits expertise.
- **Successful Entrepreneurs** - It's important to build your "tribe" of other successful entrepreneurs to brainstorm and collaborate with. Networking is especially important for solo entrepreneurs.
- **Virtual Assistants** - This is a way of having someone who is able to perform a variety of administrative support on a flexible basis.
- **Freelancers** - Working with freelancers is a great way of expanding your team. You only pay for the services you need. They offer a variety of services ranging from web design, marketing, graphic design, copywriting and others.

"For me, the most fun is change or growth. There are definitely elements of both that I like. Launching a business is kind of like a motorboat – you can go very quickly and turn fast."

- Tony Hsieh, Zappos

CHAPTER 21

Why is Small Business and Entrepreneurship so Important?

An important part of the American Dream has been that a man or woman could choose his or her own career path and rise to any height that individual desired or was capable of, provided that person was willing to pay the price in time, talent, money, or whatever else was necessary to attain those goals.

Sometimes the American Dream meant opening or getting started in a small business. It is what the pioneers thrived on and it became the major vehicle for upward mobility for thousands of people from every ethnic, social, religious and educational background. It became a conduit to a better life for the poor, the immigrant and the economically deprived.

In the marketplace, small business has increased the number and types of goods and services offered. It has been a showcase for unique and varied talents, and it has enriched the communities it served. Thousands of small business entrepreneurs prosper because they provide a product or service at a quality level that cannot be duplicated by mass production or mass distribution.

Communities have recognized the varied contributions of small businesses as well as the stable jobs it offered. In small businesses, young people often found their first jobs whether part-time, after school or during vacation periods.

Americans have always needed challenges and many seek those challenges in small business. The personal need for achievement, recognition and autonomy may not be met by employment with a large company. Small business offers open-ended opportunities to satisfy such needs.

We must not underestimate the importance of entrepreneurship in our community. Entrepreneurs impact the community in many ways including:

- Spending money
- Volunteering
- Providing jobs
- Providing a tax base
- Providing social value
- Challenging conventional wisdom
- Taking responsibility for change

If we as citizens do not realize, support and patronize these businesses they will fail to exist!

Acceptance speech given by Mark Burwell while receiving the Wisconsin Small Business Advocate of the Year Award by the Small Business Administration in Milwaukee, WI

"Entrepreneurship is a craft. You must practice and continue to cultivate your garden."

CHAPTER 22

The Power of 92

Over the last four decades I have been involved with helping the non-profit and for-profit sectors become more entrepreneurial. This meant earning their own income, managing their assets and marketing their organizations at the same time emphasizing and achieving community social benefits.

Building community wealth strategies have been around for a long time. But our culture has changed to solve our social and economic problems.

Legendary Green Bay Packer and NFL Hall of Fame player, Reggie White and his wife Sara, had a vision of empowering aspiring entrepreneurs to realize their dreams of owning and operating their own business. I mentioned to Reggie that we were missing a phenomenal opportunity to do something incredible. In 2001, we accepted the challenge to not only teach a man to fish but to change the fishing industry. This new frontier or sector meant evolving a viable ecosystem of programs and to be a community co-axle for social enterprising to exist.

The vision manifested into an outstanding foundation of empowered entrepreneurs who have developed self-sufficiency and now feel a sense of giving back that is necessary to the free enterprise system. After Reggie's passing in 2004, I named his legacy, the *"Power of 92"*, which was his jersey number as a Green Bay Packer.

This model has had a great success in several other communities to effect positive change. It has proven to create immense economic, social and cultural benefits. It involves educational, government, non-profit and private enterprise. After being professionally involved with all sectors, I realized that this engagement has had and will continue to have many challenges.

Some of the challenges have been:

- We lack an ecosystem to really support what we do. We are put in a box. Hopefully our new name will define our identity more.
- Tax and regulatory structures do not support many non-profit efforts.
- Enormous chunks of tax capital and donations are being used non-productively by other organizations on so called entrepreneurial growth.
- We are grappling with a shift in community wealth as well as loss of personal and business wealth from donors and sponsors due to tax incentive changes.
- Lastly, it is the vision as a community we must all share. The different cultures diffuse our meaningful goals at times.

"Hold yourself responsible for a higher standard than anybody else expects of you. Never excuse yourself."

- Henry Ward Beecher

CHAPTER 23

Economic Gardening

Why are small businesses important? They are our true job base! They are part of our ecosystem that firmly exploits innovative technology and the new economy. They are also more focused on the local market needs.

I have worked with hundreds of budding entrepreneurs who had solid jobs, but each recession they saw the economy changing and were glad they prepared themselves and didn't take the attitude of waiting for things to change. The key element was that they had to begin a different journey. To help in their journey they were nurtured by "economic gardening."

City councils, government and economic leaders push to get big business to come in with subsidized tax incentives. But this must be balanced out for existing small businesses as well.

Although many partnering resources are needed, there is a formulized fertilizer that is needed to cultivate this bumper crop of businesses.

The E-Hub model we developed has gained interest from several other communities. It takes many ingredients to make it come together. High unemployment areas that relied on big business are accepting the model.

Some of the biggest obstacles to economic gardening tend to be political. It has to be nurtured on a long-term effect. Sometimes politicians want short-term solutions.

What we must do to encourage economic gardening:
- Believe in and support our budding entrepreneurs. This means buying their goods and services as well.

- Identify the champion entrepreneurs who are expanding and adding jobs for incentives, like what has been done for larger businesses and developers.
- Don't just concentrate on start-ups, but help businesses "parent" their business. This means cultivation of second-stage entrepreneurs.

Public officials, businesses and citizens alike need to give recognition. It requires a mix of good programs, a good quality of life and a culture that encourages people to take risks and start new ventures. If this is established, the benefits of social enterprising are great.

Bad public policy can cripple entrepreneurship. If the price of failure is too high, commerce and economic activity will become fizzled. Resources must become more accessible.

Three-Legged Approach
- Growing new businesses
- Retaining existing businesses (must support)
- Recruiting new outside businesses

We need to become *participants and not spectators.* Community leaders cannot guarantee success or prevent failure. However, it is their responsibility to provide the encouragement, necessary tools and knowledge to succeed.

As citizens we must support and patronize small businesses or they will fail to exist. Some city leaders will continue to recruit for big business, which is all right, but cultivating our existing businesses will keep a lot of money, talent, wealth and resources in our communities.

America's first farmers were true entrepreneurs. They had to plant the seeds, cultivate and water, then take the harvest to the marketplace. With time, they also had to evolve just as all entrepreneurs must do.

CHAPTER 24

"Heart Power"
Our Compass to the Future

In Vince Lombardi's final speech before he passed away, he shared with his audience the concept of "heart power," that if you capture the heart, you've captured the person.

We need to support leaders who have **heart power** to look for the well being of our communities. These leaders must be accountable for creating a strong and connected community.

Leaders are found in many forms, coaches, politicians, teachers, and officers in the military, astronauts, pastors, supervisors and CEO's. Tomorrow's leaders also need to include parents, social entrepreneurs, business mentors, innovative thinkers and more.

I have been fortunate in meeting and working with many inspirational community leaders, and have had the opportunity to mentor many of them.

How do we define a community?

It is a sense of belonging... it is becoming a stakeholder and a true citizen, not just by voting but by **engaging**. Being a participant and not just a spectator; engaging in our principle goals as well as bringing passion, empowerment, creativity and innovation to the community.

How do we engage our leaders?

We must be open to respect, trust, social responsibility and giving back in our communities. Our community leaders must foster a sense of citizenship that promotes this ownership and accountability. This will foster new leaders.

We must embrace strong leaders who are new to the community, and not just born and raised in the community. They will bring in a fresh perspective that will foster growth and keep the community from stagnating. If they act as investors, stakeholders, and innovative creators, we need to welcome their ideas and accept them as contributors to the future of our community, and not just strangers.

"Have the courage to say no. Have the courage to face the truth. Do the right thing because it is right. These are the magic keys to living your life with integrity."

- W. Clement Stone

CHAPTER 25

Entrepreneurial Cupiding©

Some of the entrepreneurial buzzwords and phrases that have evolved recently include building relationships, networking, matchmaking, making the connection and relation management. Essentially, all of these phrases represent the same thing: The ability to generate more value by working together.

Entrepreneurial Cupiding© is a phrase I crafted several years ago as a business architect to place businesses and people together not as referrals but as commonalities.

With relationship building it is a given that you need to connect with others for relationships to work. Figure out what you have in common with people and businesses and build from it. You need to focus on who you connect with the most, which are usually businesses and people with common interests, skills and experiences. Connecting people and businesses is a principle that is taught and encouraged in our program to help build a *Community of Entrepreneurship.*

As you get to know these people and businesses you connect with, you will start to build a peer-to-peer relationship. Many times you share the same customer demographics and market segmentation. These commonalities will enhance your relationship and connect you on an even deeper level. At the same time these various people and businesses are an even more important part of relationship building. As long as the chemistry is right, you will learn to cupid and connect people to make successful business relationships.

Part of the cupiding© process is doing a triage of finding the specialist as well as making the introduction. These may include working in a common industry or supportive role.

Using leverage to instill a sense of what I call cooperative competition and not cut throat and destructive competition will bring many strong relationships.

At times you need to reach out and give back. The cupiding© concept does not allow for a selfish gain.

Personal bonding is a key to deepening your business relationships. You must be genuine and want to form common objectives. To keep your business relationships, you must learn how to build your trust through good communication and finding additional commonalities.

"The path to 'what's in it for me' will take you into sand traps. Believe in connecting together for a collective effort. Take a leadership position by having a shared attitude and giving recognition to all who deserve it."

CHAPTER 26

Engaging in the New Demographics

Innovative communities are vibrant when they nurture entrepreneurship and engage in diversity, new lifestyles and culture. Our communities today are the most diverse in U.S. history.

Our leaders must become champions for diversity. Many organizations, including ours, are recognizing the efforts of **Making Diversity Work**. Great challenges are there but great opportunities will reside in communities that pass the ball and get everyone into the game. If the price for failure is too high, economic growth will fizzle.

It must not be based solely on entitlements but by recognizing our champions of diversity.

Just some thoughts...
Outsiders who became insiders created America. These insiders are now afraid of outsiders.
Diversity should not be about counting heads but instead about making heads count.
It is not about representation but about utilization.
Our leaders must understand and leverage each person's uniqueness.
Diversity is a framework that has a voice.

As a community of entrepreneurial businesses, we must engage in the new demographics. Successful integration of diverse individuals depends on the successful establishment of systems and cultures that focus on the needs of our citizens – whoever that citizen may be.

Businesses that foster continual learning will draw together people of different nationalities, cultures, ages, physical needs, sexes and perspectives. We tend to have tribal paradigms and an anthropological urge to belong to a tribe. Hats, sweatshirts, photos and pictures have no place in a professional environment. Wearing your heart on your sleeve can cause a multitude of problems in a multicultural society.

Business owners and managers must stress the need to develop a strong business culture that understands individual behaviors and rewards leadership that trains and welcomes all types of individuals. We need to develop long-term orientation and a buddy program that explains diverse cultures.

As a leader in building a community of diversity through entrepreneurship, the E-Hub has:

Embraced a vision of diversity and innovation
Encouraged and taught minorities to develop self-sufficiency and not entitlements
Encouraged change outside of your comfort zone
Developed a solid code of business ethics
Raised the bar in the workplace

The new consumers are real and have a strong influence on buying power and our business success. We must reach out and serve the underserved!

"Intelligence is the ability

to adapt to change."

- Stephen Hawking

CHAPTER 27

Do You Need a Business Coach?

More small businesses and entrepreneurs are turning to business coaches to gain an edge in today's ever-changing business climate.

Business coaches are not consultants that you work with on a particular marketing, operational or technical problem. Coaches are not therapists who help with emotional issues. Business coaches should do exactly what athletic coaches do, which is to help make the most of your natural abilities and work around your weaknesses. They should make sure you live up to your goals and focus on improving your leadership skills.

I have found that many entrepreneurs are excited about navigating their own course, but sometimes miss having a boss. After mentoring hundreds of businesses, the one thing I insist upon is that entrepreneurs develop an enterprise team. This team should be made up of paid and unpaid business mentors, coaches and advisors. How can you tell if you need a business coach?

- **You're feeling stuck** - An experienced business coach can give you perspective and open your eyes to other opportunities and channels that are available to you.

- **You need accountability** - You may have established goals when you first started, but life happens and you have become overwhelmed with the day-to-day operations.

- **You want to develop new skills** - Leadership isn't the only skill you'll want to develop as a business owner. To keep your business moving ahead, you might need to develop skills in negotiating, finance or a new technology.

Beware of coaches that want to tether themselves to you. The purpose of coaching should be to teach and empower you as an entrepreneur. The challenge is to find the coach that best suits your goals and ways of doing business. Check references, interview and ask for a trial period. Remember, a good coach can reboot your business and help guide you in a new direction.

"You have to look at leadership through the eyes of the followers and you have to live the message. What I have learned is that people become motivated when you guide them to the source of their own power and when you make heroes out of employees who personify what you want to see in the organization."

- Anita Roddick

CHAPTER 28

Overachievers – The Force
That Drives Businesses

Overachievers are the relatively few men and women in companies who are innovators, participants and not just spectators. They are the true *action takers* that drive our businesses.

Through counseling hundreds of new entrepreneurs, I have found that most did not leave their company because of pay, but because they were frustrated with not being able to innovate or overachieve. In many cases, a project manager or supervisor was insecure about their success and therefore failed to empower them. As a result, companies have lost many quality employees.

One of the reasons for the increasing entrepreneurial growth in women and minorities is because they have learned the freedom to act in an independent business. They take risks, but they have a longer time frame in which to try new ideas without being fired. They still pay for their own mistakes, but are free to guide their next intuitive decision without an unsupportive manager or boss to hold them back.

Based on the experiences and observations I have had while helping grow entrepreneurial businesses, I found that these characteristics define an overachiever:

- **Passion**
- **High dose of energy**
- **Innovation**
- **Optimism**
- **Team player**
- **Sense of humor and persuasiveness**
- **Wisdom and common sense**
- **Courage**

Overachievers may occasionally be frustrated or even fired, but it is these spirits that gives them resiliency, tenacity and drive to become re-employed where they can achieve more. They work harder, waste less time, strive to improve, read more, and view less television, and do not believe in entitlements and live life to the fullest.

As an All-American runner, I realized that the more energy that you burn to achieve, the more that becomes available to you. Energy in this respect is like passion and passion to achieve has no boundaries.

The overachiever sleeps better because they sleep from physical exhaustion and not from boredom. They live longer and are in control of their lives through determination, innovation and empowerment to take action.

The overachiever shows a willingness and desire to accept more responsibility. Company leaders must recognize these attributes. Staffs should be able to make decisions without a condescending response or fear of their job.

The task of finding and developing an overachiever is perhaps the most important thing a leader can do. Presidents and owners must realize that mentorship is not an expense but an investment. It is an essential part of the professional development process.

We cannot accept a spirit of jealousy and job insecurity. Successful companies must foster and build an environment that honors our overachievers.

CHAPTER 29

Talent and Incentive Performance:
A Framework for Success

When tough times hit we look at cash flow, market analysis, inventory control and operating expenses, but measuring intangible employee talent cannot be overlooked.

One of these aspects that we need to measure is employee talent. Before companies lay off staff, restructure or hire, they need to look at intangible types of employee talent.

In the past, important measures included production, employee turnover rates, and efficiency and customer satisfaction. As we approach the new knowledge economy, the evaluation of this talent will become very important. We also need to address leadership, ethical value, technology skills, creative passion, and communication and learning capacity.

Measuring return on talent will be the true return on investment for many businesses. People drive performance that as we know, will be a framework for success. This needs to be emphasized in our educational process as well.

Important note:
To recruit and retain good talent, I want to emphasize one management aspect that works during recessionary periods,

Employee incentive performance measurement.

What is this incentive program?
Ability x Motivation = Performance.

This can be defined as a planning activity designed to motivate people to achieve predetermined organizational objectives.

Incentive performance programs are recessionary proof. While we cut operating expenses and marketing costs, employee incentive performance programs help drive business growth. They can have short and long-term results. Evidence does show that incentives drive the bottom-line. It tends to have a ripple effect on long-range profits.

Well-designed employee incentive programs are important during tough times because they can hit target markets. Marketing to mass markets during these times can be expensive and risky.

"People drive performance – that, as we know, will be a framework for success."

Incentive performance can be flexible and helps employees engage with one-on-one strategy.

Most small business entrepreneurs and many businesses have no expertise on formal design for an incentive performance model, but need to get in the game of it.

Most owners and good entrepreneurs know that their best asset should be employee talent. In other words, *good people are the key to a strong business*.

"Management is doing things right; leadership is doing the right things."

- Peter F. Drucker

CHAPTER 30

Outsourcing: The New Entrepreneurial Opportunity

We continue to witness the loss of jobs as corporate America downsizes and the budgets of government agencies are squeezed. Outsourcing is becoming the word for efficiency.

Part of todays growing sector is business services. Many have found that it is not just about part-time or temporary help, but instead a sustainable entrepreneurial business. We should praise this new phenomenon. I have encouraged many people who have been a victim of being downsized to seize this entrepreneurial route. One example is a county surveyor who lost his job because of downsizing. He went through our entrepreneurial training series, graduated and started his own surveying business in his field of passion. His family, career and new business stayed in the New North region and our community as a valuable taxpayer and talent.

Several of these cases and success stories occur each year. Some look to a new endeavor, others follow their passion, and some find a job or career after learning the basics of networking, business management, innovation and empowerment.

There have been dozens of various entrepreneurial enterprises in business services and commercial areas that capitalize on outsourcing.

We have retained hundreds of jobs and families in the community due to this outsourcing opportunity. The cupiding© concept I have referred to in the past demonstrates how these businesses, who are taking advantage of outsourcing, in turn hire and outsource other business for their own business enterprise, thus creating more economic development. They also are avoiding the headaches of taxes, harsh regulations and mandates of hiring employees.

In the next decade there may not be as many corporate high-rise buildings, but instead budding small businesses and entrepreneurs sprinkled throughout our communities.

Finally, as the business grows, take a lesson from the businesses that outsource. Know exactly what your core business is and let the entrepreneur specialist in their field do what they do best by outsourcing.

CHAPTER 31

Broadening the Pond of
Entrepreneurial Leadership

Leadership is important when creating an entrepreneurial climate. Below are the responses to some of the questions I have received during my talks on leadership.

Are leaders born or made?

- Preparation *(Champions do not become champions in the ring – they are merely recognized there)*
- It is a process *(Many facets make a complicated process)*
- Talent is only one aspect. Formal training widens your knowledge and gives you experience. Next you master your role *(Vision, strategist and administrator)*.
- Sacrifice *(Not just a one time payment – giving back)*
- Communication
  o Belief in people
  o Relationship – honesty
  o Accountability
  o Approachability
- Raising the Bar *(Achieve quality and excellence)*
- People must buy into you and then your vision

How do you empower people and encourage them to use their talent in your business? Anyone can steer the ship but it takes a leader to chart the course.

- Start a course of action
- Be willing to take a risk – expect challenges
- Adjust priorities
- Teach them to become mentors.
  Raise the bar for them and get them outside their comfort zone.

Create activities and events, and then observe:
- Who leads
- Who inspires and leads
- Who passes the ball

How do you motivate the unmotivated, or can you? Most people fail to recognize the value of leadership.
- Most think it is for only a few
- Few people take leadership classes or seminars
- Teach people that leadership is a process

Learning doesn't just happen; it takes years of hard work. Everyone wants a quick fix or a snapshot. If they do not add value move them out of your inner circle of decision-making.

How do you motivate and help people overcome resistance to change?

- You must inspire them as well as share your vision, mission and values.
- Have them set goals for the organization as well as themselves. Then have them do their own reviews and time study analysis.

As we grow older we protest change, particularly change for the better. By empowering, constant change is encouraged. Encourage innovation and stimulate new ideas.

What do you look for when you recruit human resources?

- Innovation and creativity
- Leadership – being a participant and not a spectator
- How do they prioritize? (time management)
- Desire and passion – this is what will help with your momentum
- Positive attitude
- Achievements

- Identity
  - Character
  - Appearance
  - Communication

Your education and knowledge are only pillars. I look at not only the outward appearance but also the heart.

How do you build and sustain a great entrepreneurial culture?
- Teamwork – pass the ball around
- Mentorship
- Monitor progress
- You must empower people. Only secure leaders give power to others. We learn to become insecure, jealous and resist progress in our society.
- Build support and trust
- Do not create barriers. Instead push them to raise the bar.
- Reward and recognize

"We all love big ideas.

If an organization lacks enthusiasm,

if the people are bored, it's time for a

big idea. The moment you set a new

goal, you crate a gap between where

you are and where you really want to

be. The urge to close that gap

generates tension, energy,

enthusiasm, purpose and drive."

- Harry Gray

CHAPTER 32

Getting Your Ideas to the Marketplace

Do you feel naked without your cell phone? How about the cup holders in your car? There was probably a time in your life when you didn't have these things. Once we have them, how could we live without them? This is the power and simplicity of innovation.

Many entrepreneurs assume their creative idea can be commercialized into a profitable business. Ideas must go through a rigorous funneling process to get to the marketplace. Diamonds have to be separated from the coal.

I recently had the opportunity to lead a panel at the New North Summit in Sheboygan, WI entitled, "Innovation and Technology Transfer: Bringing Your Ideas to the Marketplace."

Most people who take an idea to the market think they need to start with a lot of money for prototypes, packaging, patent fees, production, sales, material and inventory. More importantly, key questions need to be answered: Is there a market for your idea? Can it be commercialized to the marketplace?

People have good ideas. The problem is they usually don't modify their idea to what the market needs or do not see the right distribution channels. Markets that do not exist cannot be analyzed. Suppliers and customers must discover them together and evaluate and research the future possibilities.

Many times people with technical or engineering backgrounds do not look at the product-to-market approach. Instead, they become paranoid that someone is going to steal their idea. Confidentiality is important, but commercialization to the marketplace is even more vital or the idea will end up on a shelf or in the dumpster. Branding the product is essential down the road.

Many hours are required with an expert in the field to keep the product or service moving. I recommend establishing goals, benchmarks and timetables.

Do not risk your entire life savings by attending a fraudulent seminar on patents that says you will get rich. There are important steps and a process to knowing if your product is market ready and then finding financial investors.

Many times you will face rejection so you truly need mental toughness like Thomas Edison. Thomas Edison was the greatest inventor of all time. He had over 1,000 patents but also had over 8,000 failures. People would ask him if he was crushed each time he failed. He would respond that he never had one failure and that he learned from every attempt, each leading to a more likely pathway and eventually a success.

Some tips to remember:

• You must have a positive attitude and persevere.
• Be open to suggestions. and understand the importance of timing.
• Cope with things that may go wrong.
• Form relationships with your advisors who may help.
• Take time to research the idea. Many universities or technical college offer research and market feasibility.
• You must be able to understand what the industry price/cost margin is to make a profit.
• Calculating a preliminary manufacturing cost and comparing it to competition is an art.
• Is the product unique and have important benefits?
• Where is it in the market product cycle?
• Are there any regulatory or licensing requirements?
• Will packaging enhance its effectiveness?
• The final question is, "Will the customer buy it?"

CHAPTER 33

Finding Prospects, Not Suspects

As consumers we have been taught, and had pushed at us to find the cheapest prices. As entrepreneurs we can't have that mindset. Let the big box stores do that and continue to offer weak service.

Small businesses are known for creating new innovative products and services. Entrepreneurs need to strive for that fresh, rewarding service and experience.

By creating the lowest price, and weak service and products you are establishing a magnet for suspects not prospects.

If people are beating down your door most of the time it is due to giving away prices. People wonder why businesses that seem to be busy go out of business. They simply cannot cover their operating costs and prices they do not cover their costs of goods or payroll. I call this a *volume trap.*

I constantly remind entrepreneurs to stay in business; they should not mess around with suspects but should go after prospects. The price-only buyer is going to squeeze every drop of blood out of you and your business.

Key reasons why you should deal only with *prospects and not suspects:*

- They are usually the biggest complainers
- They want you to throw in the "extras"
- They do not want 100% satisfaction but 125% and still are not satisfied
- They usually are notoriously slow payers
- They are negative complainers to other people
- They usually are time-wasters they want to squeeze you and then they want to think about it.

- They brag to your other potential prospects that they got lower prices. This tends to absent your good customers who pay your solid prices.
- They steal your ideas, customers and knowledge when they can.

Beware! Don't worry about customers that buy only on price. They are not loyal. Don't be held hostage on prices. Be proud of your prices! Understand the economies of pricing. Learn to understand your formula for your break-even points. Remember you pay yourself and your loans back on profit margins not just sales.

If price was the only reason we bought things you would not need marketing or sales staffs. Get your customer to refer clients to you for having great service and products not just price. *What clients and customers really want are not just low prices!*

Customers want:
- On time service or delivery
- Selection and options to compare
- Product or service quality and features
- Great customer service and experience
- Respect and courtesy
- Help in making their decisions
- Reliability and dependability
- Predictability and warranty
- Follow-up and appreciation
- The best value
- A handshake, smile and a thank you

We also as entrepreneurs cannot abide by the theory that Waldo Emerson Thoreau stated . . . "Build the best mousetrap and people will come". *This author was never a business person.* We need to add in the recipe for correct pricing and of course be passionate about customer service.

CHAPTER 34

Social Enterprising

Many companies tap into the needs of their consumers to have a positive impact on their communities. I continue to emphasize to entrepreneurs that is not just having a strong product or service, but how your business practices good citizenship. That advice can be also be applied to non-profit organizations.

While the heart of non-profits is a social benefit, the need to become financially strong to sustain their mission is equally important. In that spirit, social enterprising helps to merge the two missions of creating social value and a revenue stream.

During the last several years working with community foundations and non-profits, it is evident they have looked at new ways to help themselves become more financially solvent. Many non-profits have a serious concern with their transfer of wealth, donors leaving communities due to retiring and moving to warmer climates with a better tax base.

Smaller non-profits and small business entrepreneurs are finding it difficult to compete with large government agencies and educational institutions that have grant writers and staffs to administer government and large foundation grants. These same larger government organizations are also competing for the business and consumer dollar.

Here are some of these concepts:

- Create a giving back responsibility as a condition of the free enterprise system.
- Empower people to gain influence over their own lives and their communities. Understanding basic financial wisdom.

- Learning to become a team: Building community strength through collaboration in order to make a true impact.
- We need to focus on reality, not fantasy. Entrepreneurship establishes self-sufficiency. This goal has to be worth the effort.
- Because leadership provides for the future, true leaders must provide hope. They must create a level playing field with creative ideas and servant hearts.
- Build a community of believers and mentors to take a role in imparting business ethics and principles.
- Become a creator of social value in our businesses to build the community; not benefiting from personal agendas.
- Recycle your services to others, whether it is time, attention, love, finances or other unique resources. This is a natural extension of feeling gratitude. In the face of this new reality, an increasing number of our entrepreneurs and non-profits are beginning to appreciate increased revenue and are becoming self-sufficient. They are reinventing themselves as social entrepreneurs and combining the passion of their social mission with a businesslike discipline, innovation, confidence and adherence that our program helps develop.

"How to never work another day in your life . . . fall in love with what you do; believe in what you're doing; strive to continuously improve"

- Bob Moawad

CHAPTER 35

Non-Profit Survival . . .
Engaging Your Volunteers

The national spotlight is on the economic stress that businesses, education and government are suffering. Meanwhile the non-profit sector as well is desperately strained. Corporate sponsorships and donations are down and volunteer talent is being mismanaged and leaving.

Many non-profits have gone to innovative ways for revenue streaming. Social enterprising has been one of those answers we advocate in our entrepreneur development series. We have worked with non-profit organizations to *think entrepreneurial* to become self-sufficient. You cannot afford to sit on the sidelines. Non-profits should look to local innovative entrepreneurs for their goods and services for revenue streaming and fund raising. It is a win-win situation.

The real need starts with recruiting volunteer talent. Technology, accounting, legal and marketing expertise are all needed. Unfortunately, national volunteer rates are declining and non-profit management has a high turn over rate. Some reasons that volunteer talent is not returning:

- **Failing to recognize volunteer's contributions, time or talent.** Not just money donors but all volunteers need to be recognized. Also recognize assignments volunteers are given. The value of volunteers is not always measured in dollars but in all the in-kind services provided.

- **Inspiring through leadership.** Non-profit CEO and Directors need to take an active role in mentorship and training. The word volunteer is sometimes taken for granted.

- **Matching volunteers to their skills.** It takes a savvy non-profit manager to work them into their strategic plan. Too often they want to hire more staff instead. I have found that having fewer meetings, and working one-on-one with these professionals, utilizing their skills in a temporary setting with staff and outside resources pays huge dividends. To often these talents end up being wasted through manual duties.

Many volunteers want a sense of belonging or connecting to the community. Directors need to get them to share the importance of the organization's mission. We are in an age of retiring baby boomers that offer non-profit expertise and a vast knowledge of professional shifts. Do not put them to work doing administrative work or painting the office. Utilize their skills!

"Non-profit leaders need to engage and expand their vision of volunteers. From this, an innovative talent of volunteers must evolve."

Many non-profit management leaders will continue down the same old path. The survivors will take advantage of the vast pool of talent or help mentor new leaders. If they can put together this talent, pool and establish some social enterprising revenue streaming they will continue to be a great asset to our communities. We must all take ownership in our communities.

CHAPTER 36

Recreating the Arts with Design Thinking

Some fine arts programs like other non-profits that serve a community cause are on a perilous path.

Attendance has changed and the median age has changed. Now is the time for a reboot.

I had the opportunity to address the Wisconsin Symphony Orchestra State Conference and brought to them some design thinking to help with what I call *cause enterprising*, non-profits and entrepreneurs working together by giving back.

U.S. non-profit arts organizations have boomed from my high school days in the mid 60's of just a few thousand to more than 50,000 today. They have also grown with more museums, theatres and leading symphonies with increased programs as well.

The Dilemma:
- Depleted reserves
- Diminished support from public sector
- Reduced giving from sponsors and donors
- More competition from other non-profits
- More people in need of your social cause

The arts median audience age has risen 6-10 years. Some arts leaders say people don't have time today. Actually, we have more leisure time by 8 hours a week.

But studies show just 10 minutes a week on the arts and that's just less than 9 hours a year. It's not financial reasons but cultural and social. We need to produce another generation of people to attend our arts. Fine arts have been slow to adjust to the marketplace.

The taste of young adults has waned in part because arts and music classes have been declining in most public schools. Technology for youth has them looking at music and art in a different way. The arts can **cultivate** the young by offering teasers on the web.

Now is the time for organizations to rethink who they are. What value do they create, which people in the market do they need to reach and how will they reach them.

Non-profits need to recognize that they are businesses too and not just causes. This hybrid is the wave of the future for both profit and non-profit companies. .

Reinvent your non-profit organization with a for-profit business approach! Non-profits have to continue to be innovative. They have to diversify their revenue streams and become more entrepreneurial.

In conclusion, innovative communities are vibrant when they are creative by nurturing entrepreneurship, accepting diversity, new life styles and culture.

"Caution! The left-brained world wants you to "be realistic" and "quit dreaming". "Get your head out of the clouds" and "be just like us." To advance and prosper, steadfastly ignore that advice."

- MARILYN GREY

CHAPTER 37

Right or Left Brain Entrepreneurs

We all have a dominant side of the brain that we tend to prefer and rely on. Most business strategy tools are based on logical means and keep left-brain thinkers in the comfort zone. The education system is also primarily designed for and by left-brain thinkers.

Right-brain thinkers are artistic and process ideas with emotion, intuition and visualization.

The right-brain person may have a difficult time in the traditional learning environment. They often become confused, discouraged and sometimes criticized for daydreaming and not focusing. This person may actually have great entrepreneur assets but doesn't realize it.

Upon doing entrepreneur assessments with potential entrepreneurs, I've noticed that most are visual learners are in the **creative class**. On the other hand, it is exciting to see left-brain mindsets take the challenge to learn how to respond visually and spontaneously to entrepreneurial challenges. Here are some of the dominant features of both right and left-brain thinkers.

Right Brain Thinkers	Left Brain Thinkers
Gut feelings	Like concrete facts
Intuition	Logical thinking
Unstructured	Clear priorities
Imagination	Focus on details
Multi-tasker	One task at a time
Visualizes the big picture	Step-by-step patterns
Internal focus	External focus

In business, it's important to engage in *creative cross training.* This enables entrepreneurs to have a more integrated approach and be able to multitask more efficiently.

Years ago I learned to displace the following myths:

Myth: Because I am a right-brain thinker, I don't do well on tests and therefore won't succeed in business.

Reality: If I prepare and practice those things that don't come naturally, business and managerial functions come easier.

Myth: If you learn business management tools from the left side it will hurt your creative side.

Reality: We not only strengthen our non-dominant traits but we help strengthen even more what we are naturally good at.

Brain exercise is like physical exercise - you need to develop it. When the weaker side of the brain is stimulated to work in cooperation the efficiency of the stronger side also increases tremendously.

In another chapter of this book, I talk about how entrepreneurs need to outsource some of their weaker skills to other businesses. This is necessary to build your capacity and be more productive in order grow your business. Don't forget - you still must learn both sides to be able to oversee and grow your business.

Doing a brain mapping assessment will help you realize what characteristics you already have, and an entrepreneurial assessment will help you realize what you need to develop. You can then move on to a SWOT analysis (strengths, weaknesses, opportunities and threats). This is what you will need for your business analysis to see the feasibility of your business. It truly is your three-legged stool.

CHAPTER 38

Women Embracing Entrepreneurship

Over the past 30 years, I have seen a nation on a brink of entrepreneurial transformation. It is not just about small business, but entrepreneurs responding to the marketplace, which evolves every day.

Women are changing the entrepreneurial landscape. They have been reevaluating their priorities, flexing their muscle on empowerment and using their creativity to help build a community of entrepreneurs.

Innovative communities are vibrant when they are creative. Communities that stay conservative or do not reward change are dying. Women are the growth engines of tomorrow.

It has been exciting and rewarding to see many alumni from our Entrepreneur Hub recognized as top entrepreneurs. There have also been many women regional business plan winners, "Make Mine a Million" finalists as well as elevator pitch finalists at a regional Entrepreneur's Connection Summit. My wife Cheri, who I refer to as a *Serial Entrepreneur,* was named the Chamber of Commerce Entrepreneur of the Year in 2006 as well as being awarded the Entrepreneur of Excellence Award by our Entrepreneur Center. She has been a champion entrepreneur for women, mentoring and empowering others over the years to follow their passion.

Entrepreneurship has been viewed as risky with no crystal ball on the promises of long-term security. Entrepreneurship has no guarantees, but working in a hostile and unsure environment also has its risks.

Women are eager to escape a confining structure. They are told to follow the rules and many times told that they can't do something. Entrepreneurship can reboot your life in a way to explore other options. It can be a great self-empowerment tool to change your life, celebrate your creativity and an opportunity to design your lifestyle. You have the ability to see your kids at athletic and school events, have lunch with a friend, take family vacations, do a workout during the day, have no bureaucratic structure and not have to worry about being downsized. This does not mean a leisure life but a balanced one.

Do not think of entrepreneurship as a sprint, but as a marathon where you have hills to go up and a pace to maintain. Adherence is important and the rewards do come.

Each of us can make a difference in the world. What we do to make that difference is our purpose in life.

Women are great at my philosophy of being a **participant** and not a **spectator**. We need to make a splash in someone's life…start a hope that moves other's lives. As we touch more people, our splash becomes bigger and the ripple effect broadens the pond even more.

Just a few of the qualities of women entrepreneurs that I have witnessed over the years:

Wisdom – Mothers and leaders. Both provide direction, vision, guidance and proficiency.

Mental Strength – Must handle the pain of setbacks and the risk of challenges. Must plan strategies, delegate tasks and follow up on the results. Then seek out how to improve.

Hopeful Believers – They develop trust in resources, family and friends.

Connectors – Women are natural connectors. I have seen many women who have connected themselves to resources they needed after having developed self-esteem and empowerment.

Entrepreneurship is isolating so you need to establish a team of paid and unpaid advisors. I like to use my term of cupiding© or connecting, which has been a great asset for women. Women have a great knack to develop camaraderie and support. This connecting is important when starting a business.

The value of social responsibility has also helped women become community leaders by giving back. Many of these entrepreneurs have become mentors, presenters, Chamber of Commerce ambassadors, and served in non-profit leadership roles to help build our communities.

"When you educate a man, you educate one person. But when you educate a woman, you educate an entire community."

"The critical ingredient is getting off your butt and doing something. It's as simple as that. A lot of people have ideas, but there are few who decide to do something about them now. Not tomorrow. Not next week. But today. The true entrepreneur is a doer, not a dreamer."

- Nolan Bushnell

CHAPTER 39

Solutions for Motivating People

I have pointed out the importance of leadership and employee motivation to reboot your company. I would like to provide a **Blueprint for People Performance Strategy.**

You must have leadership and teams that work together to experience success.

Define an Effective Team:
- Accomplishes tasks/objectives within a time frame.
- Are team members happy and have a stake in the project?
- Production is a measurement for accomplishments.
- Communication is frequent and clear.
- Respects each other's roles.

Team Building:
- Draws on everyone's best contributions. Creates synergy to help facilitate a winning team.
- Continually evaluate your team and coach them.
- Look for leaders - clarify roles and boundaries. Look for performance rewards on those meeting your goals.
- Provide growth opportunities that are flexible according to employee's talents and diversity.
- Do not accept incompetence– always stress accountability.
- Act like a family.

Every organization needs performance in three areas:
- Direct results
- Building of values
- Building and developing people for tomorrow. I have found cross training to be my favorite and productive word.

Team Leadership:

- A leader is the one who makes you want to work hard and makes you feel good because you did it.
- Create an environment for people who want to do their job, and not have to do their job.
- Leaders are action doers; they have the vision and inspiration.
- Leaders are mentors– trust and strengths capture everyone's trust, dedication and respect.
- Act like a family.
- Show solid business ethics and values.
- Managers are driven by daily operations – leaders by the future. Leaders are long-term thinkers.

Strong Clear-Cut Mission Statement

- Employees must know your mission statement!

Goal Setting

- Goals should be from a position of strength, not desperation.
- Having a lot of great archers and shooters does not do any good if they do not know where the target is.
- Get everyone involved with short-term goals.
- Be community involved!

Technology Strategy

- Find a clear purpose. All managers do not need to know technical details about information.
- Right now, technology has many employees and customers very frustrated and productivity and personal relationships have gone down.

People Performance Management

Leadership – This provides the vision, attitude and passion of the organization. Management style is to "inspire" and motivate.

Training and Development – Foster an understanding of your goals and objectives, and training to meet those goals.

Communication – Face to face, newsletters, meetings and intranet.

Employee Relationship Management – Integrate external and internal marketing concepts. Motivating employees toward Customer Relations Management.

Accountability – Measurement on return on investment needed. Customer retention, sales, profitability is key.

Technology – Company intranet helps with interrelationships and communication to provide reference and training information.

Rewards and Recognition – Put a strategy in place.
- Reward your trainers and mentors
- Build champions – they are not made on the field but deep inside with desire and vision.

Performance Incentives – Rewards

Incentive – Stimulating one to take action, work harder, encouraging, motivating.
- Incentives impact people's performance.
- Fewer than 25% of all workers are working to full potential.
- Cash is not the best motivator. This leads to entitlements.
- Incentive programs need to be well designed.
- A leader turns problems into excitement.
- A leader empowers people to make decisions to develop a high power organization. Leaders show people what they need to do.

State Your Feelings and Expressions During:
- Important meetings
- Yearly recap
- Holiday messages
- Employee speeches

"Reward solid solutions instead of quick fixes. Reward risk taking instead of risk avoiding. Reward innovation, not status quo. Reward intelligent work, not busy work. Reward team building."

CHAPTER 40

A Customer-Driven Vision: The Missing Ingredients to Satisfy the Customer

I have spoken to several firms and companies on how important customer service is, but it must start from the top. The company must have a *Customer Driven Vision.*

You need to develop a win-win mentality:
- Preventive – knowledge power from staff
- Focus group – customers
- Management establish customer-driven vision

Outstanding service will set you apart from competitors. Learn what they want and how to deliver it. Do not wait for complaints. Customers and clients want, options, information, knowledge, understanding, courtesy, patience, resolution, availability and fairness.

The following are important ingredients that I would implement to help the non-satisfied customer.

Step 1: Have the right attitude
- Perception is reality. The customer will always be right in his or her own mind.
- Assume that the customer is being truthful with you. Do not search for, or point out, flaws or holes in their story.
- Remember you both want the same thing –you are not enemies.
- Think of the complaint not as a battle of right or wrong, but a problem solving session.
- Get all the ghosts out of the closet.

Step 2: Prepare to take the heat
- Don't get defensive.
- Gather the information by listening. You will need all the information to resolve the problem.
- Do not interrupt or add comments until the customer is finished. Keep your cool.
- Let the customer defuse emotion by speaking and explaining the entire situation. *Note:* Delegate interruptions to someone else so that your entire attention is devoted to the customer. An interruption increases the anger and frustration felt by the customer.
- Never use the words: "It's our policy."

Step 3: Demonstrate that you are going to help and show empathy
- Let the customer know you empathize with how they feel or were treated.
- Reinforce what you say by using your tone of voice and body language.
- You don't have to agree. You don't have to admit guilt. But do express understanding.

Some examples might be: 'I can understand how you feel.' or 'That might make me a little upset, too.' And 'Let's see what we can do about this.'

Step 4: Before you end the interaction, make sure you understand the problem
- Ask for clarification if the facts are not clear.
- Make sure you understand the entire situation without jumping to conclusions.

Some examples might be: 'So that I can best help you, let me be sure that I am clear on the facts.'

Step 5: Provide a creative solution to the problem
1. Do what you can to solve the problem. Sometimes you have to ask, 'What would you recommend as a fair solution?'
2. Provide options instead of saying no.
3. Do not reflect anger or make the customer feel guilty about having a problem.
4. When the situation is resolved, both you and the customer should feel good about the resolution.

Step 6: Invoke a 24 to 48 hour follow-up
- Thank the customer for expressing their concern as they leave.
- Perform any follow-up actions promptly.
- Follow-up with the customer after the fact, even if not required, telling them the action is complete.
- Apologize when appropriate.

Step 7: Show the customer you are accountable
Make sure the problem is brought to the attention of the person who can fix it.
Document customer complaints to identify trends.

"Better communication can solve problems. The best employees prevent problems rather than just solve them."

"Listen with curiosity. Speak with honesty. Act with integrity. The greatest problem with communication is we don't listen to understand. We listen to reply. When we listen with curiosity, we don't listen with the intent to reply. We listen for what's behind the words."

- Roy T. Bennett

CHAPTER 41

Time Wasters and Energy Vampires

What do we all have in common with famous successful people like Bill Gates, Oprah and Tiger Woods?

We all have 24 hours in a day, 7 days in a week and 365 days in a year. Whether it is in sports, art, business, inventions, politics or science, all the successes have come from people who only had 24/7/365. We all have a level playing field with time, even during all our athletic events.

But it is what we do with our time that makes us the winners, or to become successful. A lot of us use the expression "Not enough hours in a day".

I have given several workshops on Time Management from the Energy Vampires and time wasters to company management and self-management goals. Entrepreneurs are always trying to *beat the clock.*

Being an entrepreneur and mentoring entrepreneurs, I explain that we all have an unbelievable way of leveraging our time, because we are in control.

People have asked how can we accomplish more? Managing and leveraging time is the biggest factor. Entrepreneurs have the control to achieve extraordinary results.

Here are some tips:

Overcoming the biggest obstacle
Being able to say no. That includes many energy vampires who want your expertise and time, without reciprocating.

I have found that during down economic periods, people tend to have more time to waste. These can become the energy vampires in your life.

Be a decision maker
Entrepreneurs are in charge, so be balanced and use your passion to enjoy and stretch days for business, socializing, self-improvement, meditating and family time.

Don't procrastinate
We all do it, but it does lead to time wasting in the end. Don't be a bystander. Don't put off mini tasks until the end of the day.

Reboot your goals
Review with yourself, your teams, staff and peers. Discard some and add new ones.

Organize, Organize, Organize
I see this the most in people who appear disorganized. They waste your time on the phone, e-mail, and especially meetings. As a trainer and consultant, I have seen administrative staff up to top CEO's who have needed help in time management.

Prioritize, Prioritize, Prioritize
Don't be afraid of tackling big or hard jobs first.

As a business architect, I have found that designing a business plan, strategic planning, short term day-to-day operations to long range benchmarks are solutions, **but only if you apply them.**

Understand time zones and time schedules
I have always made sure that I make my early contacts from the East coast, and later contacts with the Pacific Time when offices are still open. I never like to call local businesses or clients during the noon hour. This is a great time to re-organize your day as well as getting small tasks done.

Time Tips:
Avoid going to lunch or dinner during peak waiting times
Avoid e-mail or phone tag

Evaluate participation in time wasting meetings
Schedule your day around peak driving times

Evaluate the best social networking venue for your time.

Get a good calendar system
The office stores have tons of options on calendars and planners, small to large. Whether you choose to use paper or an online system, choose one! Then establish a system that is organized, productive, portable, and most of all, one that you are comfortable with and will utilize. Use it to schedule your personal and business time.

Do an annual analysis of your time. I always feel that it is like a report card, but also like a bonus reward to show that the wasted time was less, enjoyable time was more, and accomplishments have grown.

The nice thing about leveraging your time is that you won't have to go to the bank to ask for more money to achieve more growth or personal time, you have earned it on your own.

"The nice thing about leveraging your time is that you won't have to go to the bank to ask for more money to achieve more growth or personal time. You have earned it on your own."

"Time is an equal opportunity employer. Each human being has exactly the same number of hours and minutes every day. Rich people can't buy more hours. Scientists can't invent new minutes. And you can't save time to spend it on another day. Even so, time is amazingly fair and forgiving. No matter how much time you've wasted in the past, you still have an entire tomorrow."

- Denis Waitley

CHAPTER 42

Beware of Procrastination

In a recent time-management seminar I asked, "What is the number one time waster"? The majority said...*interruptions.* This is a good answer, however I find that procrastination is the real dilemma. Insufficient or ineffective planning are key components to wasting time.

Interruptions are a part of life and will always happen. Procrastination is mostly a lack of self-discipline and goals that are not clearly defined.

Time management is an important part in the act of controlling your day-to-day activities or long-range goals. Organization is a skill that can be learned. The key to getting better organized is to start with one small step and then take others one at a time. From there, persistence and follow-up are keys to consistent organization. Create a framework on your decision-making processes.

As an entrepreneur, when your business is going well you will work harder and longer hours. But you must also focus on your vital priorities. Procrastination will tend to lead to unproductive time thus not finishing your daily projects or long-range goals.

"Procrastination is mostly a lack of self-discipline and goals that are not clearly defined. Draw from the past, see the relevance on the present and anticipate the future."

A great leadership and time management theory I have always used is goal setting. A goal is an anticipated event that you want and wish to bring into your control. To do this, draw from the past, see the relevance on the present and anticipate the future.

It works the same way in the business world as it does in your personal life. Draw on the past, control the present and project the future. As you work on your goals you put values on them, thus managing your time. Do not always do the easy tasks first and put off the major jobs. This only puts out the fires. Avoid this type of procrastination. It will only get you further behind.

Strong leaders tend to control the amount of procrastination and have good time management skills. They are like farmers because they know how to cultivate the people around them to develop a team and reap the harvest of the future.

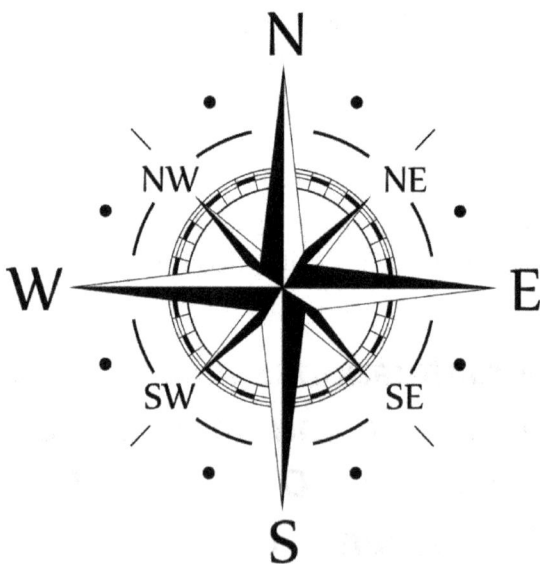

CHAPTER 43

Let's Get Back to Business

Refining Business Dress: Image Management

After teaching many different leadership traits, image is one that is very important.

Image management is the ongoing process of evaluating and controlling the impact of your image. The resulting response is creating an appropriate, authentic and attractive personal and professional image, which increases your confidence, credibility and productivity. It contributes to the success of you and your business.

Logic of a Professional Image:
The way you look effects:
>The way you think
>The way you act or behave
>The way you feel
>The way others respond to you

Benefits of a Professional Image
Value to the Individual:
>Improved communication
>Increased confidence
>Increased competence and capability
>Increased credibility
>Increased creativity

Value to the Business:
>Improved communication
>Increased consideration and civility
>Increased cooperation and loyalty
>Decreased tardiness
>Decreased complaints and litigation
>Increased quality

Increased productivity
Increased sales

Are you casually confused?
It was thought that the business casual phenomenon in the early 1990's would enhance the morale, creativity and productivity of employees within all arenas of the business world. What has been observed instead is a decline in office decorum as a whole. Along with casual attire has come a casual "kick-back-and-take-it-easy" attitude.

Many companies across the country have noted that on dress down days there is a decline in productivity, a higher degree of tardiness and absenteeism, more flirtatious behavior and a general sense of relaxed demeanor on the part of the employees.

It is obvious that casual dress is not a fleeting trend, but an ideal that is here to stay. Confusion occurs when the definition of business casual is unclear. It is certainly not the intent of any employer to increase productivity by allowing sloppy apparel in the workplace. However, those who do not set an appropriate example and who fail to clearly define what their expectations are regarding casual dress, set themselves up for a potentially catastrophic decline in employee commitment, loyalty and quality of work. Although it may seem elementary to those authoring the policies, it can be very destructive for them to assume that employees know the difference between leisure wear and business casual wear.

In order to be a winner in the game of success, you must be fully aware of the ways that you can present a powerful image for yourself and the company you represent based on the clothes you have chosen to wear. With the traditional business suit being worn less frequently than in times passed, it is even more crucial to know how to be as authoritative in professionally casual attire.

CHAPTER 44

Innovation to Impact

If you had to draw a picture to describe the meaning of innovation, you would probably draw Thomas Edison's 150-year-old light bulb innovation that is on the front cover of your program. But due to the innovation of LED technology, the incandescent light bulb will soon become a thing to remember in the history books.

Our current culture is teaching our kids to stay inside the boundaries and we force our employees to stay inside the box. What we have done in the past is not going to work in the future. We must be **shepherds of innovation**. Small, innovative and adventurous steps will get you there.

Many of us have taken these steps. Sometimes the American Dream meant starting a small business. It is what our pioneers thrived on. It became a conduit for immigrants and a new social-economic culture. That is what we stand for.

Innovation starts with the analysis of opportunities. Nobody loves a downturn, but many successful entrepreneurs say that they have become innovative, aggressive and launched their business during tough times. Some examples have been Adolph Coors, William Wrigley, IBM, UPS, General Motors, Walt Disney, Hewlett-Packard, Domino's Pizza, Super 8, and Microsoft.

Business never stands still – innovation, new opportunities, challenges and realities are drivers to success. The competitive landscapes are always shifting.

Innovation is not limited to technology, but also the ability for those to see opportunities in the marketplace and recognize unapplied value. Many of our entrepreneurs were downsized at some point and took the opportunity.

Innovation is your tool. We have presented it to you as a discipline capable of being learned and practiced. Only you are capable of going out and applying it. Step up to these new opportunities. There is no other option!

Navigating this course can be challenging but rewarding as many of you have found out.

"Don't be the one who says, 'It was my idea'. Be the one who takes it to the market and profits."

CHAPTER 45

Entrepreneurs Need to be Shepherds of Innovation

Are you cutting costs to survive or promoting more than ever to keep your business alive? The rules and playbook have changed. Today, you truly need to reboot your business by evolving through innovative change.

For small business entrepreneurs trying to get through our latest economic and financial crisis just lowering costs and treading water won't be enough.

Here's my dose of expertise to become the new "Evolutionary Entrepreneur":

Don't innovate for the future, but for the present

Respond to customers changing values. This may be new products or service opportunities.

Keep it simple and focused, not confusing, and **start small.**

Review your business model for different distribution channels.

Look through different lenses of different industries for options.

Understand the turbulence of how doing business in the marketing and technology areas will change dramatically. Old ideas from advisors may be passé.

Think about a new customer base. By using innovative change you may find various niches you never realized.

Clients and the consumers will pay the price for **unique products** and excellent service.

Communicate with your customer – don't just sell or market to them.

Don't assume that your supplier's advice is always on target.

Don't be content if sales are okay now. Be **aggressive** and not **complacent**.

Pioneer a new field every year. You need to **position yourself** as a leader in your field.

Build on social responsibility to your community.

Create an experience in your business: Teaching demos, etc.

Add value to your product or service. As costs go up you must maintain your profit, but by adding value raising your pricing won't be realized.

Don't stop being innovative.

BURWELL'S TREND RESPONDING MODEL©	
10%	New Innovative Products or Services
20%	Trend Responding in Industry
40%	Basic Products or Services
10%	Related Products or Services
10%	Promotional/Value Oriented
10%	Bundle or Tier Pricing

Just remember to never put all your eggs in one basket.

CHAPTER 46

Economic Impact Yardsticks

New yardsticks are needed to measure the true long-range growth as a better way to track our economy. We need to measure this through our entrepreneurial and innovative impact.

We see the plethora of economic data and statistics, but they seem to be measured by standards of the old economy. These reports that are assembled by the academia world, business leaders and government economic developers may not be what drive our future entrepreneurial and innovative economy.

We need to revamp our current statistics to track what data is needed to boost the economy's long-range growth potential. Some of our current statistics are meaningful, but many are redundant and looked at as short range. They were created to track the old ups and downs of our economy.

The new data should change how we perceive the economy, putting more emphasis on design, technology transfer, product and service development, entrepreneurial innovation and other intangibles that drive growth and jobs. This should then in turn influence economic policy and funding.

Sometimes entrepreneurial start-ups and failures are part of the innovative cycle, but their statistics are sometimes misunderstood.

In an economy where we value innovation and creativity, we need to adopt new tools to measure this impact.

This must also be done within the business plans that are produced. This entrepreneurial innovation will create change and more economic value. It helps us respond to our new culture and diversity, generations and lifestyles. Venture capital and investment financing is one way to measure this.

I realize that financial institutions need hard assets to be used as collateral, but we need to be competitive and find ways to fund innovation when it is in the building stages, which sometimes has risks involved. The stock market is a risk as well as a corporate job. Life is all about risks, but to be too conservative and wait is also a risk.

Small entrepreneurial start-ups, innovation, intellectual property and solid management must also have the tools of external financing help just like the promises of large projects that tend to look good, but also stumble and fail.

Our national, state and regional leaders want us to develop higher paying jobs, but it is also really about a chance for entrepreneurial financing and investing as a hope for our long-range vision and growth.

"There is a spiritual aspect to our lives – when we give, we receive. When a business does something good for somebody, that somebody feels good about them."

- Ben Cohen, Ben & Jerry's

CHAPTER 47

The Emotional Change Journey

Change is a part of the evolutionary business process that an entrepreneur experiences. It is a natural emotional path that occurs. Many times this change challenges people with ideas or concepts.

In the face of these challenges, people often act to undercut the change. I have found that leading by inspiration is the best way to get through this time of emotional journey.

I recommend three steps and actions to help lead through these changes.

The first phase is the greatest challenge, creating a feeling that there is a need for change. Make everyone feel that they are still in control of their environment. Start to plant some seeds.

The second phase is getting out of the comfort zone. There may be resistance, anger or even fear. People may feel uncertain and anxious. You must learn to listen to fear or anxiety and not confront or bully your way through it. Continue to respond to these concerns while moving forward with your journey.

The next phase can be designed into the change itself. I have found that you can actually design many of the concerns into the transition process itself. It tends to engage everyone using innovation as well. This engaging tends to get everyone into focusing on the future.

Once this happens, you should not look back. In this phase, everyone will start to connect the dots to create a game plan to answer the many unanswered questions that still exist.

Next you will need to give direction but without stifling anyone's ideas in the process.

The last phase is commitment. Once the changes are tested, shaped and molded, solutions will take shape at the end of your emotional change journey. These solutions will start to restore direction and stability. This is your sign of acceptance and commitment. People who resisted the change start to realize the opportunities and benefits.

As an entrepreneurial leader, it is always important to share with everyone your vision before, during and after your "change journeys."

CHAPTER 48

Surviving Growth Traps

Survival is an issue that entrepreneurs are seriously concerned about. Many of the entrepreneurs I have helped over the years have concerns with marketing and launching their business, but not managing your growth can be a major concern in the long run. Some key advice on avoiding growth traps include:

Putting automation before customer needs
If you install new computers or other automated services but cannot fulfill your customer's needs, the transition period can hurt you tremendously. Sometimes businesses worry too much about cutting costs that it interferes with the quality of service to customers. The customer does not care if you are installing new equipment.

Losing Your Creativity
Find what you are going to do to make yourself different. You have to conduct market research in order to find your own niche, which is the creativity. You have to create excitement in your business.

Failure to Change
Surviving growth has a lot to do with change. A company may want to sell the same product but if the competition has taken over the market, the company has to do something different to survive. Growth is not necessarily the same as success. You can still remain small and compete.

People also have to become **intrapreneurs** rather than entrepreneurs to compete nationally or internationally. We need to be more innovative. The United States is good at creating things and not copying others. In the state of Wisconsin, we tend to have a good work ethic however we also need to expand our creativity.

Ignoring Employee Talent

Employees can provide a window of opportunity and businesses need to recognize that as a resource. The key is that companies have to work with their people and use their talents. Use them as a network to the community. Many businesses go out of business because they did not know what the customer wanted. The problem is that management is too busy looking at trade journals and interested in making more money than listening to its sales force or other employees who have closer connection to the customer. Employees serve as a focus group. Knowledge is really a human resource. It cannot be found in books. When employees feel good about themselves they produce good results.

Taking on the Wrong Risk

Startup businesses can take on the wrong risk by not appropriately identifying if a market for their product or service exists or by not understanding the market. The number one reason people go out of business is they were in the wrong business to begin with. Sometimes the person feels they can start a business where they do not see a business or product in a market, but they do not realize that type of service is not in demand or the product lifecycle is over. Many people plan to start a business for something that is hot now, but by the time they get into business, the demand for the hot product is over.

The Volume Trap

One small company that made a quality CD holder started out making about 200 products in its own plant to sell to specialty stores. Then the company accepted an order for several thousand more products from a mass merchant and had to subcontract the work. As a result, the overhead went up and quality went down. The company then lost its position in the market. In addition, the company received another larger order from the mass merchant, supplies were ordered but then the order was canceled, which forced the company out of business. Everyone thinks they want to sell to Wal-Mart and make a million. In reality it only ends up being a trap.

The Geographic Trap

In expanding a growing business, some companies tend to expand in a place too far away. When a company expands in another city, for example, it will have to deal with different things such as different regulations, distribution channels and a different work ethic. A lot of times you are going to a market you do not understand.

"Every human has four endowments; self awareness, conscience, independent will and creative imagination. These give us the ultimate human freedom - the power to choose, to respond, to change."

- Stephen Covey

CHAPTER 49

Survival Tips and Identifying Red Flags

Entrepreneurs still need to identify key red flags to survive. This is one of several checklists that need to be reviewed periodically:

Failing to spend enough time researching the business idea to make certain it is feasible.
Many entrepreneurs fail because they are under-capitalized or have the wrong people. However, the most important mistake is that their original concept was not viable.

Miscalculating market size, timing, ease of entry and potential market share.
Most new entrepreneurs get very excited over an idea and do not look for the truth about how many people will want to buy their product or use their service. They put together financial projections as part of a presentation to hype up their investors.

Underestimating financial requirements and timing.
Many entrepreneurs will make a commitment to a certain amount of office space, a number of computers, hire too many people, and so on. Before they know it, based on sales projections that were wrong to start with, they have created costs that require those projections to be met. They eventually run out of money.

Over projecting sales volume and timing.
Many entrepreneurs miscalculate the size of the market and over project their portion of it. When you break it down, a much smaller number of the market is actually sales prospects. This is what makes it impossible to make your sales projections.

Making cost projections that are too low.
Crunching numbers in a realistic budget of revenue and
expenses is very important. An example is hiring too
many people and spending too much on equipment and
facilities.

**Lacking a contingency plan for a shortfall in
expectations.**
Even if you are realistic in your estimates, there are
things that happen when you start a new business. Your
sales ideas might not be good and bank rates may
increase. These are not the result of poor planning, but
they will still happen.

Hiring for convenience rather than skill requirements.
It is hard to fire people, especially if they are relatives or
friends. More time needs to be spent hand picking
people based on skill requirements. You need skilled
people who can wear more than one hat.

**Accepting that it is "not possible" rather than finding a
way.**
If you are an entrepreneur, you are going to break new
ground. A lot of people are going to say it is not
possible. A good entrepreneur will always find a way.

**Volume trap: Focusing too much on sales volume and
company size rather than profit.**
There is too much emphasis on how fast and big you can
build a business rather than how much profit it can
make. Bankers and investors do not like this.
Entrepreneurs are into creating and building, but they
also have to learn to become good business people.

**Seeking confirmation of your actions rather than seeking
the truth.**
Entrepreneurs will talk to friends and family about an
idea they have. However, they are only looking for
confirmation and not the truth. Give more value to the
truth than to people saying what you are doing is great.

112

Neglecting to manage the entire company as a whole.
This happens all the time. Entrepreneurs will spend half
their time doing something that represents five percent
of their business. You have to have a view of your entire
business and see the big picture.

Whether you are starting a business or currently own or operate a
business, learning by your mistakes can be expensive.

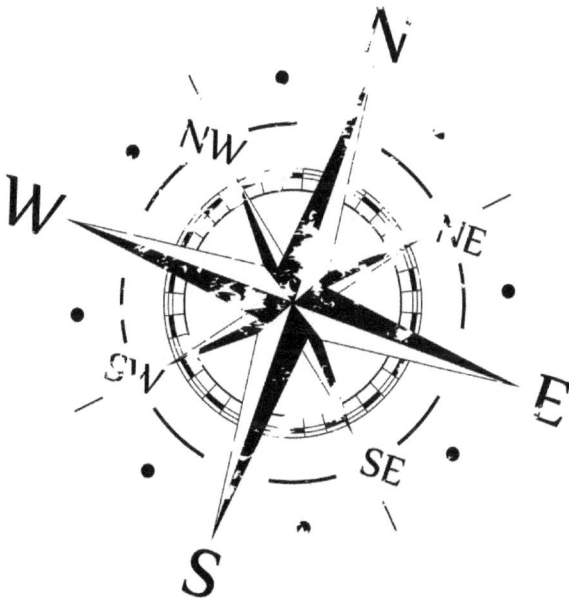

"Goals give purpose.

Purpose gives faith. Faith gives

courage. Courage gives enthusiasm.

Enthusiasm gives energy. Energy

gives life. Life lifts you over the bar."

- Bob Richards, Pole Vaulter

CHAPTER 50

Don't Trip on Old Myths

The talk on the street for years was that the government should run their business like big business to be more efficient.

Maybe both government and big businesses need to take some tips from small business entrepreneurs. Rather than pointing fingers, it maybe time for all organizations to get their house in order.

Faced with an unpredictable economy at times, we need to review old myths and wake up to new realities. Free enterprise shakes out the weak and non-innovative during a recessionary time.

Here are some mistakes and myths to stay away from to remain ahead and on the leading edge:

Thriving on Chaos
Putting out fires is not good. It draws energy, hurts planning and kills relationships and morals. It takes you off your vision and mission.

The Sale is the Solution
Making the sale is the end result as I have said in several of my previous articles. But, the true solution to business success is forming strong relationships, which builds into true assets. The sacred commission may be an immediate solution, but you still need long range goals to maintain your existence.

Keeping Both Eyes on Competition
I tell entrepreneurs to be aware of competition and not afraid of it. Several of our peer-to-peer mentorship relationships are business competitors working with each other.

The key is to be more innovative and better visionaries. Just because your competitors are doing something doesn't make it smart, effective or right. Shadowing competition is only a lack of self-confidence.

Making a Quick Buck is Important
Cash flow is important but offering a product with no service will catch up with you. Organizations that make an investment in the future and a commitment to their customers and communities will be around for a long time. Our organization advocates social enterprising, which in turn empowers people, businesses and communities.

Getting it Done is More Important than How it Gets Done
This is probably one of the only times I will suggest that finishing first isn't always the objective. Don't ignore how the job gets done via professional matter, image or expense control. You need to project the best image possible even if you finish second or third.

Your task now is to be more innovative, passionate and run faster than your competition. Keep your eyes on your long-range vision and not just short-term solutions.

CHAPTER 51

Managing Downturns

Running or managing a small business often leaves little time to keep track of national and even regional, economic indicators that might affect your industry and your specific operation. Conditions such as interest rates, inflation, gross national product, stock prices and consumer confidence have direct impact on your profitability and on relationships with vendors, customers and even employees.

During periods of economic decline, whether widespread or cyclical for a particular type of business, entrepreneurs are most likely to bear the brunt. The fact that conditions are changing opens up opportunities for resourceful businesses to outsmart larger competitors who, during a downturn, carry on business as usual or are unable to adapt quickly.

Such innovative small firms can:

Gain market share by taking it away from competitors unable to adjust to shifting market conditions.

Maintain a strong cash stream throughout the downturn, in contrast to other companies that may have liquidity problems.

Become a leader, more cost-effective and more efficient operation, better positioned to do well when the market improves.

The challenge is to be aggressive and imaginative. Entrepreneurs who survive and even prosper during hard times must be able to look beyond the present, to overcome the constraints of tradition, to see the firm from a new perspective, and to do business differently.

Here are some recommendations for small businesses:

1. Watch your inventories carefully, but do not hold them down so tight that you lose sales.

2. Monitor your cash flow very diligently and forecast it monthly to ensure that expenses and planned expenditures are in line with accounts receivable. Make sure your financial statements provide information that is timely, relevant and accurate.

3. Separate the *nice to do* from the *have to do*, and eliminate nonessential expenses as much as possible.

4. Watch the credit worthiness of your customers, even bread and butter accounts. Remaining close to existing customers, and checking to see how they are getting on during the downturns not only helps avoid unpleasant surprises but could also lead to new opportunities.

5. Get aggressive with collections.

6. Strengthen your banking relationships.

7. Do not skimp on service and quality by being understaffed. Options include freelancers, consultants and part-time employees.

8. In strategizing how to build your customer base and induce current customers to raise revenues, the importance of good service cannot be overstressed – especially as their buying power or willingness to spend is lessened during tough economic times. Studies show that perception of service is fixed primarily in terms of time in a customer's mind. Three examples are: waiting time to obtain service; reaction time to deliver service; and length of time of the service.

9. Advertising survival guidelines include:
    Monitor your competitors' advertising.

Center your message on the benefits and advantages of your product or service.

Stress quality and durability.

10. Training can be best conducted during slack periods – especially low-cost, on-the-job instruction and broadened skill acquisition.

"The fact that conditions are changing opens up opportunities for resourceful firms to outsmart larger competitors."

Get employees involved in policy choices as well as tactics and implementation. Meet with staff regularly to exchange ideas on boosting productivity and other issues. Create an incentive for good suggestions and foster a team spirit for survival. Remember that employees need to feel they are important to your company.

Resourceful entrepreneurs identify and capture the available opportunities and take steps during today's hard times to lay the groundwork for tomorrow's prosperity.

"One of the greatest discoveries a man makes, one of his great surprises, is to find he can do what he was afraid he couldn't do."

- Henry Ford

CHAPTER 52

Overcoming Fear During Tough Times

Many economic developers, media, financial institutions have approached me, and of course, the general public, regarding what it takes to start a successful business during the recessionary tough times. My answer to them is simply this. . .

It is really the same as during thriving times; **passion** innovative ideas, a solid business plan, honest business ethics and values, cash flow, and overcoming **fear.**

Many of the entrepreneurs that I meet with have confidence, but want the crystal ball prediction of their success before they even start their journey.

To minimize the risk and overcome some of this fear, the main ingredient really boils down to one word…. **preparation**.

Setting goals and meeting those benchmarks is important. There tends to be more start-up entrepreneurs during recessions because they tend to be more fearless and go against all odds at times – but this also means more opportunities.

Deep down there is always the **fear of failure** for them, but there are others, such as:

Competition is another fear for small businesses. My key tip here is to be AWARE of your competition but not afraid of it. You will eventually work on an innovative niche to become successful.

Fear of the economy has always been on our minds throughout history, but not an overwhelming fear like it has been in 2009. Sales and credit are tight – the important note to remember is that some of our most successful entrepreneurial endeavors in the past have been during tough times. We tend to be prudent during these times, watching expenses and customer service more.

Fear of being alone – you must develop a focus group and an enterprise team, which I have mentioned in previous articles as a support mechanism. Some entrepreneurs actually fear being in charge, so having an advisory team can boost confidence and reinforce strategic plans. Surround yourself with peers and never be afraid to ask for advice, *but remember to take it!*

"Overcoming fear of failure by entrepreneurs brings on empowerment and strength in the long run."

We all have many common fears including spiders, snakes, heights, public speaking, and yes, doing a business plan.

Many of us will never become entrepreneurs because we will never take that risk of self-sufficiency, but in today's world, working for someone else is also a risk.

CHAPTER 53

Opportunities in a Crisis

What happens when the stock market is falling flat on its face and politicians are giving no assurances as to what may happen? What are our hopes and aspirations in the near future?

During many past recessions and economic downturns, I have told many small businesses and entrepreneurs that when there is a crisis there is also opportunity.

Some points to consider:
It's a buyers market! We are in the age of the consumer. They are feisty, self-reliant, time sensitive and very smart.

Their message is, "you meet my needs."
Those needs: Selection is fresh; staffs are knowledgeable, pleasant environments, convenient locations, parking, hours, web presence, internet access and creative solutions.

Even though the economy is on a downturn, consumers and businesses are exercising their voices through their pocket book. It is not just about bargains, but quality and convenience.

As an entrepreneur you must:
Continue your vision and leadership in your niche – emphasize your strengths.

Search the marketplace for the most innovative goods and services to bring to your market.

Update how you do things through technology.

Review your webpage.

Start or continue to improve on community service. Many times giving back to the community will lead to profitable opportunities.

Hire the best, innovative people you can afford.

Formulate focus groups to ask them what opportunities you can provide.

Consider now a good time to reposition yourself in the marketplace so when the economy improves you are ready.

Communicate more with your clients or customers via a newsletter or social media.

Lastly, develop or improve on your Customer Relationship Management (CRM).

Build on the most precious asset you have - your existing, loyal customers. Don't ever take them for granted! As a matter of fact, they are your stakeholders so in a crisis, they will probably be your best opportunity.

"In a crisis, be aware of the danger,

but recognize the opportunity"

- John F. Kennedy

CHAPTER 54

The Road to Today . . .
The Journey to Tomorrow

I believe that each of us has a dream placed in our heart.

As I witnessed graduates come through our entrepreneurial programs over the years, I witnessed the vision from their hearts. To many, it was the thing that they seemed born to do. I could see the talents and assets beaming from them. They were looking for the compass that sparks to continue their journey. For many, it seems to be their purpose in life.

Showing you how to establish vision, good character, business ethics, and surrounding yourself with a solid enterprise advisory team aren't always taught in the books or online.

Building the hope for your journey is what Reggie White believed in. The "Power of 92" is all about empowerment and staying in the game, not just being a spectator.

Life is a one-way street! You may take a lot of detours but none take you back. It may sometimes mean facing detours. . .this is called fear and failure, but it's all a part of life.

"Your dream is a journey, not a destination."

"Look around you. Everything changes. Everything on this earth is in a continuous state of evolving, refining, improving, adapting, enhancing, and changing. You were not put on this earth to remain stagnant."

- Dr. Steve Mataboli

CHAPTER 55

We are Evolving Faster and Faster

Since the Industrial Revolution, we have been moving faster and faster. We have built a world on innovation. It is what our entrepreneurs thrive on.

We are in a society of change. It is accelerating and it is not going to slow down. Sometimes marketing and technology changes take us out of our comfort zone.

In my workshops and presentations, I explain that you need to have the word adherence included as part of the definition of the word entrepreneur. Resiliency is more important than ever.

The challenges of our economic climate, escalating work hours and financial uncertainty have been hard on all sectors of small business.

These stress levels can burnout business owners and entrepreneurs. Add to that the polarization of government, technology change, competition, regulatory reform and healthcare costs and we have a whitewater rapids effect.

To cope with these rough waters:

- Adopt a positive approach and mindset.
- Look for new opportunities.
- Train yourself and your staffs or you will be caught in the middle.
- Pace yourself. In the long run it is a marathon and not a sprint.
- Go outside of your comfort zone for change, but wear your life preserver.

- Understand the new forms of industry markets, marketing channels and technology.
- Be aware but not afraid of your competition.
- Build on your network and connections. Build a strong "enterprise team."
- Be flexible but stay on task.
- Get outdoors, exercise and get your rest.
- A healthy diet needs to be learned and followed.
- Your family and spiritual well-being can be your best partner going through your challenges.
- Believe in the values of solid business ethics. Be a civic leader and give back to your community.

Warning: Do Not Swim Alone!

Always know where your compass is. Learn how to plan, map and take the right paths. Your journey will be much easier.

CHAPTER 56

Using the Ripple Effect to Broaden the Pond

Myth: If you do what you love, money and fortune will follow.

Reality: Following your passion is important, but it's beyond the passion where you need to understand and identify your entrepreneurial skills and talents.

Journey: Research an entrepreneurial and enterprise team and interview yourself.

Ask yourself these questions:
- I've always wanted to do what?
- What do I value most?
- What is my purpose in life?
- What value can I bring to a business?
- What will make me a community leader?

Measure these questions against your passion. Next, you need to explore your personal entrepreneurial qualities.

Ask yourself these questions:
- What do I excel in?
- What do people compliment me on the most?
- What comes naturally to me?
- What am I good at?
- What am I burnt out on?
- What skills do I need to develop?

Measure these questions carefully and hone your skills toward the future. Now, form your vision, your sense of purpose and ethical values. The vision will be hard to pursue if your team has unqualified skills. They all need to contribute to your strategic plan.

Once you have your plan in place, you will need to grow the business to a solid profit base and build your own business model.

This is done successfully by **broadening the pond.** Think of it as throwing a stone into a pond of water to create a ripple effect. The pebble is you as the visionary. You then turn into a mentor, sharing your sense of purpose, the company mission, vision and values. This cultivates people and truly finds rewards for all the players on your enterprise team and staff. Having a collaborative effort will reap the reward of success.

When following down your paths, always look for opportunities and not just the fires you need to put out. You must be prepared! Have good people in place, show good character, have a product or service that fits the marketplace and a plan that shows the ability to re-pay your lenders.

"On your journey to becoming an evolutionary entrepreneur, don't just love what you do, do what you love. Evolve. Look for ways to reinvent yourself in your job, your business, and your life."

CHAPTER 57

You Cannot Afford to Fear Innovation

Change and innovation can often times be a paradox for small, medium and even big businesses. Many owners and managers know that they must take a journey down a different path and change direction before they hit a dead end. Non-profits and small businesses tend to be in this group as well. They feel change is too risky, takes time and resources. Major corporations like GM are also stubborn on change.

Innovative entrepreneurs and organizations cannot afford to not embrace innovative new roads. Entrepreneurs need to embrace the unknown rather than fight uncertainty.

Research shows that a large percentage of innovative projects or program changes are successful. Yes, stepping into innovation is a step into the unknown. It creates fear of failure. Entrepreneurs and managers must set out to sail even though an iceberg may be in the distance.

As an innovative entrepreneur, you may want to shift a portion of your money and resources to the business or organization of tomorrow.

It takes sometimes two to three years to develop a new concept and turn a new profit and revenue stream. You need to get out of the starting blocks. Many entrepreneurs or managers wait until it is too late. They continue to take their products and services down the same lane only to see their competition pass them by.

Analyzing the industry and market properly before committing resources to developing new products or services can solve all of these problems.

Get your head, or team, out of the sand! Carefully assess the market needs and get an intuitive sense at what the need for customer solutions are in their businesses or arena.

Do not be a trend driver or follower. *Be a trend responder.*

"It takes an understanding of the customer and client's needs for you to rally the troops so all the players are in to succeed."

CHAPTER 58

Creativity
The New Currency for Success

Many of us are following a myth - follow the policies, learn a skill, work hard and you will be taken care of.

The workplace has not always proven this to be true. Technical skills are important, but they are just one aspect to being competitive, especially as an entrepreneur.

Our marketplace continues to evolve with economic challenges, fierce competition and quicker time to respond to our client and customer needs.

I have stressed in the past: *"Evolve . . . reinvent yourself."* Do this by making creativity a priority. American creativity is continuing to decline!

Our answers seem to come from our computers. Too often I hear, "I have been told that it is not the way it is done in my industry." How can you become an entrepreneur and get to the next level if you cannot reinvent and explore through new innovation?

"You need courage to break the mold and interrupt the status quo."

Your competitive edge is your creativity. People who can imagine new alternatives to tough solutions increase the impact that their companies can make. They are rewarded and go beyond the boundaries.

Break out of the vanilla box! Start with the environment around you. Do not become institutionalized. Your workplace must produce some creative flow. Boring cubicles, vanilla offices, yellow florescent lighting, meetings, meetings and more meetings, spread sheets and no windows does not set the stage for a creative physical environment to work in. Creative motivation does not need to be a major expense.

My experience has seen people and organizations turn their backs on change out of fear. Many watch the world go by. Success, I have found, passes through stages. The first is criticism, next the journey and then seeing proven results of success by innovative change.

Here are some important tips to breaking through the barriers to entry into the marketplace:
- How do I beat my competition?
- What are the obstacles and challenges of the current industry and how can I improve it.
- For existing companies, reboot by listing creative ways to break through stagnation.
- Spend 10% of your time and energy on new creative products or services for the future.

"We must reward the risk-takers, innovators, creative thinkers, and doers!"

CHAPTER 59

Broadening the Pond During Tough Times

It takes a special person to be entrepreneurial and to become a good manager of growth.

You must **broaden the pond,** meaning you need to enlarge the pond you fish in. It's all about going after market share. Do not expand the pond into an ocean but a small lake. That way you will not sink your boat.

Tips for entrepreneurs in tough times:

1. You need to keep a cool head.
   - Use your connectors such as your advisory enterprise teams.
   - Communicate often and openly to assure the right steps are being taken.
   - Take time to plan a restructuring strategy.

2. Do not become complacent. Keep the pressure on.

3. View tough times as opportunities to re-establish your way of approaching your mission.

4. Focus on solving your problems and not on trying to blame someone or something.

5. Have your company on their toes during good times so when times change you are ready.

6. Learn to benchmark your strengths against top performers outside and inside your industry.

7. After reviewing other business leaders, do not be afraid to raise the bar even more.

8. Simulate stress through scenario planning. Review ups and downs that could happen. This can help identify your gaps and actions you have to address.

9. During tough times as a leader, here are the two most important factors to consider:
- Ease anxiety and stress
- Provide a path for yourself and employees to identify priority issues and meet challenges to solve problems.

10. Replace large formal planning processes into more frequent mini-sessions.

Always remember, that during tough times, sustainability is more important than growth.

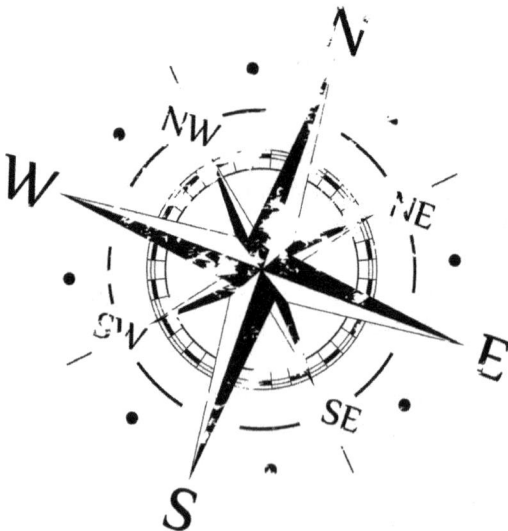

CHAPTER 60

Speeding up the Strategic Learning Process

It's not about a long-range plan in today's world. One of the most common threads we see in our business is reinventing our strategic planning.

- Getting the most out of our employees.
- Getting them to follow your vision and mission and making sure you adopt a good strategic plan to drive the execution of your goals.

In your entrepreneur leadership roles you should make strategy everyone's job. Some companies and organizations tend to set aside retreats to do their planning. I tend to call them *advance strategy* to reflect a new aggressive vision and strategy that would inspire and not demand.

Traditional planning focuses on a strict plan based primarily on quality. In today's competitive environment, we need to be concerned with speeding up the velocity of strategic learning. Speeding up the process, pausing to analyze our results and taking corrective action lets us claim new strategic insights, which allows the learning cycle start over. Successful companies will keep the learning wheel spinning as fast as possible. The faster we can prioritize these strategies, convert them into decisions and translate into actions, the better we are to win the race.

Getting commitment and performance from your staff is important. A large company recently contacted me about finding good people. Their business was declining; they did not have a recent strategic plan or external or internal training program.

They said they were letting their "dead wood" go and could not find people. My response was, "in order to get the right people on the bus, you need to create a bus worth riding."

A solution is to establish what I call a **Mentor Advantage** concept, which I will explain in future chapters. Fill your company with coaches and not bosses. Leaders are skilled at helping people do their very best on production and achievement. Reward the guides as well as the productive employees.

Because of job insecurity and a faulty management style, this can be a huge challenge. Any challenge can be turned into a great opportunity, which in turn builds successful companies.

I have seen first hand companies focusing on developing people rather than just looking for them. You need to identify the diamonds in the rough in and outside your business.

"Leaders should influence others in such a way that it builds people up, encourages and edifies them so they can duplicate this attitude in others."

- Bob Goshen

CHAPTER 61

Why Goal Setting Often Fails

Many entrepreneurs need identify the road to get to their successful outcomes.

Goal setting fails not because of lack of talent, money or motivation. It is because a sense of purpose was not shared and objectives were not stressed. No follow through or proper monitoring was done.

The difference between entrepreneurs who get their desired results and those who do not starts with setting up the pillars of a business plan: Vision, mission, value and philosophy statements.

As you parent your business, you start to establish a strategy called strategic planning. While it takes time, you need at times a coach or mentor to help you establish your strategy, which defines key employees and managers. You must be a participant and not a spectator in the process.

The more the business or organization grows, the more you will grow and develop as a person, so keep learning!

Not having a coach or mentor will result in not achieving your goals, lost time, stress and mismanaged resources. Important factors to consider:
- You need to see the big picture.
- Have a journey that is prepared for bumps in the road.
- Do not ignore uncertainties.
- Do not live within a management by crisis environment.
- Do an analysis of your competitive landscape.

Following your strategic plan breaks down your goals.
- It helps you make decisions on the go – in our ever-changing, evolving business environment.

- Communicate the plan to others.
- Be ready for opportunities that come along.

To define, remember that your objective is what you want to achieve. Your strategy is how you plan to achieve, and tactics are action steps to take to reach your strategy.

Without a plan it is easy to go in many directions. Your strategic plan must have measurable outcomes.

What I recommend to growth and expanding businesses:
- Establish goals outside your comfort zone. Examples: Learn to blog or partner with non-profits to establish social enterprising.
- Establish a list to shed your "non-performing" items.

"Our goals can only be reached through a vehicle of a plan, in which we must fervently believe, and upon which we must vigorously act. There is no other route to success."

- Pablo Picasso

CHAPTER 62

Market Segmentation:
Getting that Special Piece of the Pie

Understanding the market you want to target is probably the most important issue in your business needs and success. The fragmentation of our customer markets today is extreme and complex.

Understanding words like demographics, segmentation, psychographics, behavioral targeting, market analysis, and GIS (Geographic Information Systems) are sometimes confusing to entrepreneurs.

Simply stated, who is your customer?

Here are some observations to understand to get that special piece of the pie:

Let's start with B2B (Business to Business)
- They are usually larger accounts.
- You have to get it right first because you may not get as many chances to have additional clients after you have reached your target.
- Big businesses are easier to find due to data that is available.

Most common target market B2C (Business to Customers)
- The consumer groups are the most difficult to dissect, find and analyze their data.
- Brands are important.
- They purchase smaller amounts.

Evaluate your competition and be aware of it, not afraid.

Market segmentation is a key strategy entrepreneurs must put into their top priority. Start-ups must take market segmentation serious or they will not exist.

"Entrepreneurs and business owners want that silver bullet, but there really is not a crystal ball. You must constantly be observing and listening to the marketplace."

CHAPTER 63

Discovering Your
Market Opportunities

In the last decade, entrepreneurial business leaders began to recognize that being technology driven was just not good enough. What came of this? **A customer-driven movement.**

We needed to understand what our customers want first, so we needed a business process improvement like Six Sigma and TQM. Innovations needed to be more efficient and taken to the next level.

Second-stage entrepreneurs struggle with:
- Not understanding the right market segmentation
- Bad data collection and analysis
- Not the right growth target markets
- Improper marketing and branding
- Missed opportunities and channels
- No business model to fit the new business generation

To discover new markets and grow your core markets you need to discover the idea of **Outcome Driven Innovation.**

Listening to the voice of the customer has been the mantra for the last three decades. This voice tends to slow down the innovation process because our customers are not the best qualified to know the best solutions. We need to get better inputs to solve the customer's true value propositions.

Our marketing messaging channels fail many times to show the true value proposition.

We need to obtain the customer's requirements that: Perform jobs faster, better, more conveniently and less expensively than before. A requirement is something that customers want or need, so solutions and benefits need to be considered.

Discovering where the market opportunities are:

Opportunity, like requirement, has been defined and redefined so many times that it needs to be prioritized more effectively. In mature markets, companies find it more difficult to discover unique opportunities. As a result they often compete on price and erode company profits by moving toward commoditization.

One way to avoid this is to be more innovative by looking at the underserved customer segments.

Who are these markets?

There is always a group of customers who are more demanding than the rest. They are called **prospects.** They are underserved in the value proposition. They want more and are willing to pay for it.

Identifying customer segments that should not be targeted:

These I will call **suspects.** They may require excessive service while demanding lower prices. Successful evolutionary entrepreneurs can identify the prospects and not the suspects.

What is the value to your customer?

Customers do not just buy a product or service. They buy value. When I put together private label programs in my business, the brand needed to build a promise of quality and not on low price.

Designer labels and identifiable labels and selection were also a value if they had the quality and were the current trend. Identify your value proposition.

CHAPTER 64

Communicating the Value Proposition

Small businesses never seem to get enough seminars, workshops and webinars on marketing, advertising and now social media.

The biggest mistake most make is approaching promotion tactically rather than strategically. You need to take the guesswork out of defining your target market.

Identifying your value proposition is the reason customers and clients pick your company. It is the centerpiece of communicating why people choose you. Yet, it is one of the biggest challenges every entrepreneur faces.

Once you create this value you need to identify how you will reach your customer base.

Before diving into your marketing strategies you need to define your niche target audience. Hitting the target is essential otherwise you will waste time, money and energy. This not only wastes your resources but can erode your sense of value in communicating your perceived value.

To be effective you need to identify your psychographics. These are values based on assessments of customers. They identify how consumers spend time, what work they do and what brands they buy.

Demographics describe education, sex, age, race and geographic location. Many small business start-ups think they want to appeal to all people, which usually results in not being anything to anyone.

In the end you need to develop your value proposition. An effective value proposition answers the questions your target audience is wondering every time they learn of your new product or service. They ask themselves, "What is in it for me?"

You need to address these questions:
- What are their needs?
- What are their challenges and problems?
- What competing products or services are they dissatisfied with?
- What trends do you need to respond to?

The answers to these questions form the basis of your value proposition.

Things to avoid:
- Stressing only about the company instead of addressing the needs of the customer.
- Old or generic promises – Example: The best, number one, personal touch.
- Promoting features of the product or service and leaving out the benefits.

Once your customers understand that you will solve their problems, you have communicated the value proposition better than your competitor.

"Vision is the art of seeing what is invisible to others. Through the use of vision and passion, we see exactly how we will win the race."

One of my expressions given as a track coach and team captain to runners as well as pole-vaulters, long jumpers and shot putters. I believe it applies to evolutionary entrepreneurs as well.

146

CHAPTER 65

Lead Generation:
Actions to Succeed

Keeping your brand on top requires keeping track of your leads, customers and loyal fans.

1. You need to build an emotional relationship.
Before you start talking to the social media technology experts you need to develop very strong emotional benefits. Promote, develop and create happiness.

2. Provide reliable service.
Dependability is your ability to fulfill the demand.

3. Experience a new design or service.
Create a feeding frenzy of got-to-have items such as gifts, trendy apparel, human and social experiences.

4. Create the demand.
Keep the public and press waiting for your new designs, concepts and releases.

5. Utilize technology and innovation.
Make sure to develop a unique and compelling value proposition. New innovation makes you a leader in the industry.

6. Create a culture.
This is the Starbucks approach. Customers like discovering new creative products. This sets you as a leader in your field.

7. Keep the customers/clients happy.
No hidden prices, restrictions, delivery costs or charges. Be upfront. Liberal return policy shows you stand behind your products and service. It is all about sincerity, openness and solid business ethics.

8. Community concerns.
You care about the environment, local jobs, employees and community.

9. Damage control.
Reputation protection. You will need to have a backup plan. For rumors, blogs or negative feedback, you will need to have a plan to distribute positive search engine optimized information.

10. Reward the loyal.
Develop a CRM (customer relationship management) program. This will help to establish a database to track your customers.

11. Build the power of "thank you."

12. Send an unexpected e-mail, voicemail or card to show your appreciation.

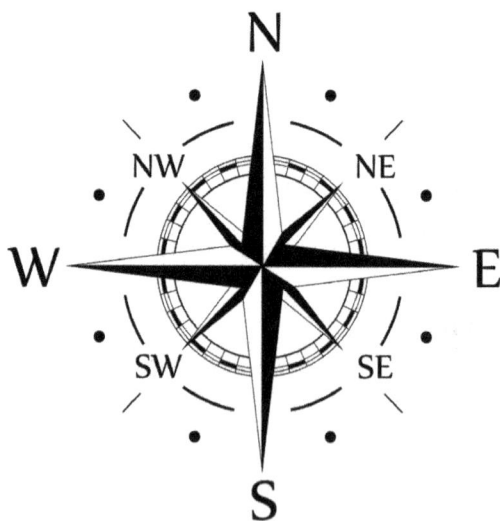

CHAPTER 66

Customer Service = Customer Fulfillment

Customer fulfillment is keeping your promise to your customer.

Customer satisfaction is all about customer fulfillment and delivering on your promise to fulfill your customers' needs through your product and services.
- Research shows that 2 out of 3 companies feel they offer superior customer service.
- Approximately 1 in 10 agrees.

What is the idea and niche behind your product or service? You must gather market intelligence, analyze and innovate to produce, fulfill and deliver.

Customer satisfaction should include:
- Functionality
- Some type of sensory impact
- Value back via performance, innovative new product or service
- Unconscious impulse
- Price/value perception
- Access, delivery, convenience

Your Product and Service Feasibility Checklist:
- Is your product and/or service readily available
- Is there a need identified by the customer
- Is it unique
- Is it protectable
- Does it have regulatory concerns
- Does it have unlimited life
- Does if have any liability risks
- Can it be expanded
- Can it be adapted for training
- Is technology needed

Measuring Success for CRM (Customer Relationship Management)
First measure:
- How many leads have been generated?

Second measure:
- How many customers are converted into clients?

Third measure:
- CRM - How long do they stay with you and how much do they purchase

Fourth measure:
- How many referrals do your customers/clients bring to you? I refer to this as *broadening the pond.*

Fifth measure:
- How many connect in the cupiding$^{©}$ process?

Quick Analysis of Customer Service:
- How are your surroundings?
- What is the value of your product or service?
- How is your customer service?

Transition into Some Solutions:
- To be customer driven, you must move away from management by crisis.
- Change from "it begins with management" to "it begins with the customer."
- Motivation comes from a shared vision and not fear or loyalty.
- Move from a decision based on judgment to doing it with duty and some performance facts.

Finally, Smash the Barriers!
Avoid the icebergs:
- Owners and managers do not always see what is below the water.
- You must ask all of your employees to help develop a quality system.
- Make a personal commitment to excellence.
- Evaluate your results.

CHAPTER 67

The New Entrepreneurial Marketing

Many entrepreneurs need to answer these questions:

- Are you in a quandary about spending more or less time and energy and resources on your marketing efforts?

- Are you stuck in the traditional 4P's of marketing?

- Do you know which customer segments are potential revenue streams and which ones are winners?

- Do you recognize the blood sucking money and energy vampires in your marketing strategy?

- Is social media the only answer?

- Are you working on your value proposition and evaluating your customers and clients needs and wants?

- Are you creating new, innovative customer service strategies?

Entrepreneurial marketing is the combination of entrepreneurship and marketing elements to create a business that is in alignment with its values, needs, wants and jobs to be done for its customers and clients.

The traditional 4P's of the marketing mix:
Product, Price, Placement and Promotion are the roots to become the new 4C's of entrepreneurial marketing:
- Co-created solutions/experiences, customized values, choice and convenience, and lastly communication within communities.

151

Defining Your Business Purpose and Reconnecting with your Vision

- Why are you in business? Align your vision, mission and values
- Using the Value Proposition Canvas to align your value proposition with your targeted customer segments
- Pricing Strategy and Break-even
- What is your competitive advantage?

Positioning and Developing Marketing Channels

- What marketing channels exist?
- What are the best channels for you to market your business?
- Exploring inbound and outbound strategies
- Resources, activities and partnerships

Customer Relationship Strategies

- How do you value your customers?
- Getting feedback from your customers
- Create your customer service creed
- Test measurement tools

Marketing ROI, Strategic Plan and Implementation

- Create your marketing budget
- How do you know if your marketing efforts are working? Measuring your success.
- Pulling it all together: Your strategic marketing plan
- Implementation, Assessment & Pivoting

3 C's for Success:

Competence – Strive to be good
Confidence – Believe that you can do it
Courage – Be willing to step from the shadow and into the light.

CHAPTER 68

Making Sure You Get Paid

Many entrepreneurs experience slow-paying customers from time to time or even worse, customers not paying at all.

Entrepreneurs work hard at producing, shipping products on time or providing time for professional services. You also expect to be paid on time.

Sometimes it's learning how to deal with excuses people throw at you like, "I didn't get your paperwork; I lost your invoice; you missed our computer run; or our computers are down." The list goes on.

Businesses need to establish a solid accounts receivable billing system as well as a collection program or they will soon go out of business.

Take the time to review your billing and collection procedures and remember, things may change during tough economic times.

Questions to review:

- Do we give incentives to fast paying customers?
- Check out the terms, materials and invoice language.
- Do you call on larger dollar amounts with balances that are past due?
- Do you have proof of deliveries?
- Do you try to work out things before turning over to collection?

Early payment means solid cash flow and less risk of account being written off at a later time. Recharge your credit operation!

Here are some ideas I have found to be effective:
- Use the telephone and e-mail vs. collection notices and letters.
- Understand their business and industry.
- Go right to the top. This gives you faster results and personal involvement.
- Watch your language and tone. Remain business-like.
- Reciprocate or barter if that helps.
- People making the sales need to be notified and help out to speed payments.
- Break-down a payment schedule
- Work with the "prospects not the suspects."

Beware of these types of late payers:

- **Honest but confused** – Explain your terms better.
- **Non-responder** – May end up being a big problem.
- **Credit-time stretcher** – Work with them. Explain to them you also need cash flow to survive.
- **No fault of their own** – This is a natural or personal disaster. Assure them you will work with them.
- **Seasonal delinquent** – Ask for their financials or recommend a bank that may give them a line of credit.
- **The true fraud** – Don't be naïve.
- **Customized products or special orders**. Make sure to get money up front. Don't just put into your inventory.

In the end it is all about business ethics on both ends:
- Demonstrate honest and ethical business standards.
- Demonstrate strong leadership standards.
- Meet your clients and customer expectations and they will move you on the top of the list to pay you.

Lastly, remember you are not a bank and you need your payments to provide future goods and services, employees to pay and the ability to provide a roof over your head.

CHAPTER 69

Housing Your Business

One of the most serious fixed-costs as an entrepreneur is a lease. A lease can lock you into a situation you may not want to be in for several years and a mortgage even longer. Site selection has become an art and a science. If you experience road construction at your business, your target will be even tougher.

Leases are fixed expenses! Understand what you are signing.

As a business advisor, I want to provide you with tools to use. Start by putting together an assessment checklist and use values from 1 to 10. The total score will give you a better comparison on your final analysis rather than depending on emotion.

Define your business needs. One of the most common mistakes retailers make is choosing a prime space and using a large amount of that space for storage and oversized office areas. Maximizing your return on investment per square footage is your first priority.

I like to use this formula:
Rent + Advertising = Cost of Space
(Return on investment)

The more relevant traffic, the less you will pay on marketing.
- For an office or retail location, you will need to be close to your trade area unless you are a destination (sought after business).
- You need to estimate your trade area and the distance customers are willing to travel.
- You will need to get traffic pattern information as well as road construction that could hinder your business from either your real estate developer or the Department of Transportation.

155

- Accessibility is important. Make sure you are assured of enough parking spaces to be in compliance with local ordinances, as well as driveways, turns and obstructions.
- Be aware of being close to high traffic events. Businesses such as movie theaters or restaurants will restrict parking for your business.
- Understand what CAM and triple-net costs are. Common Area Maintenance (CAM) costs such as snow removal and landscaping as well as property taxes on top of your base rent will add on to your expenses.
- Competition and demographics of your customers.
- Hours of operation.

Beyond the Location:
- Have an energy audit done as well as looking at the past energy bills.
- Access for freight delivery and pick-up is important.
- Security and safety of the building and area should be investigated.
- Easy accessibility to dumpsters and trash receptacles.
- Telephone and Internet service availability.
- Physical features and renovations needed.
- Image of area is important.

Building construction:
- Is there a firewall if you are adjacent to a restaurant?
- Are there smells and/or noises coming from other businesses?

Have you checked with your insurance agent for a location analysis and liability limits? Once you have found a suitable location, does the air conditioning, heating, electrical, and plumbing work properly? Is it handicap accessible? Make sure you obtain an environmental report.

Lastly, are there expansion possibilities? By spending the time upfront to research all of these areas, you will save yourself resources and stress in the long run.

CHAPTER 70

Mentoring . . . Passing It On

In this book I explain the importance of finding a coach and forming an advisory enterprise team. The chapter on cupiding© explains why having a mentor may focus on developing the whole person and their business.

There are many kinds of formal and informal mentoring relationships from employers, schools and other programs.

The informal peer-to-peer or mastermind group has been a successful concept in practice. It is an informal journey of mentorship from the classroom to working with peer entrepreneurs and professionals. Business knowledge, social capital (paying it forward by working with non-profit organizations), spiritual support, business ethics and leadership are all part of the teachable moments. The mentors in turn get to show leadership by giving back to the community. Many are champion entrepreneurs who volunteer with other alumni, therefore, passing it on.

A strong trust must exist with commonalities where they gain strength from each other.

Tips for the mentoring process:
- Working with a program designed to match entrepreneurs may eliminate unsuccessful relationships.
- Clarify the role, time and enjoy the commitment.
- Being mentored by several mentors, even if you receive only one nugget of valuable advice.
- Respect the mentor and let them know when you take action.
- Thank them and pass on your lessons learned to someone else.
- Mentoring relationships change over time so re-evaluate.

- Mentors should not be bosses; their role is to listen and give you the hands on information to inform you to make proper decisions.
- Mentors are not your parents, friends, or your investors. They need to be objective.

Finally, having a good mentor can help, launch, grow or reboot your self and business. A bad one can shut you down. The mentors who will make a difference are not just the ones with the credentials, but the ones with your concerns.

Choosing a Mentor...What Should I Look For?
I would ask myself if I would want my children or a good friend working with that person. In other words, is this a person that would be a good role model?

"One of the greatest values of mentors is the ability to see ahead what others cannot see and to help them navigate a course to their destination."

- John C. Maxwell

CHAPTER 71

How to Choose a Mentor

- Evaluate your needs. You may need a mentor who understands your stage in the business. If you have already launched your business, you need a mentor who has gone through the start-up process.

- New entrepreneurs must seek positive leaders and role models.

- Make sure you get an advisor.
  o **Mentor** – Overall visionary and strategic planner
  o **Consultant** – You have a specific problem to solve
  o **Professional coach** – Helps you out of a slump, time management, or personal challenges
  o **Mini-Mentors** – an outsourced business service that helps empower yourself.

- Mentors may be paid or unpaid.

- Engagement is important.

- Build on your pillar of knowledge:
  o Mentors can be found in the educational system through faculty.
  o Technology and specific expertise may be found from students.

- Mentors must understand:
  o Partners of trust
  o Must be positive with a sense of vision and humor
  o How mentorships work

- How to monitor your progress
- Help you empower yourself
- Should not create barriers
- Recognize your success
- Take you through the journey of challenges
- Know how to pass the baton – they must be a compass

Your mentor should be a guiding force…with a sense of humor, good heart, knowledge to continue to learn, and someone who we show mutual respect.

"The teacher is more important than what he teaches."

- Karl Menninger

CHAPTER 72

Mentor Advantage Process

Seed Mode	**3rd grade – 9th grade** Junior Achievement models have worked well. Teaching methods to teach the creative student the process of entrepreneurship.

Cultivating Mode	**Post Secondary** Partnerships with entrepreneurs and their businesses in their respected majors Outreach mentor is field advisor with business and the students

Launch Mode	Build an enterprise team Mini-mentors needed in specific and technical resources

Parenting Stage	Specialized education, workshops, seminars Establish an advisor round table Peer-to Peer mentoring Learn to mentor

Expansion Stage	Paid outsourced resources needed in specialized fields. Establish mentors through vendors, education and outside resources.

↓

Evolve: Innovation and Reinvention	Outside consultants, coaches and mentors to help build business models. Foster internal mentors and intrepreneurs. Collaborate university resources for innovation.

↓

Mature Stage – Engage	Connect with the cycle by giving back and cupiding© (connecting) with the seed cycle

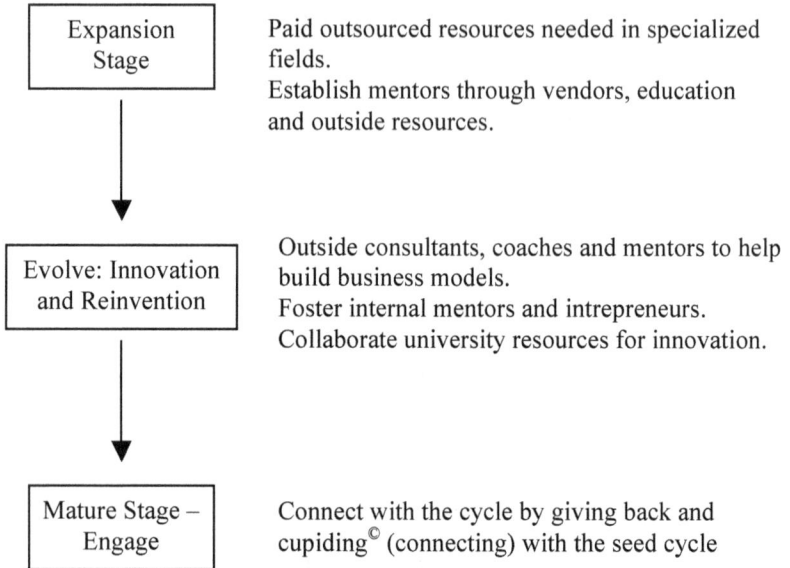

*Model was introduced at the Wisconsin Entrepreneur
Conference at the University of Wisconsin Whitewater, 2012
Mentor Advantage Model by Mark Burwell, Business Architect*

*"By mentoring you see the world
through a different perspective, and
see more than what you teach. By
bringing your wisdom and skills
you also receive great insight."*

CHAPTER 73

Salute to Minority Entrepreneurs

A few years ago I had an opportunity to lead a panel of minority entrepreneurs at a Green Bay Chamber of Commerce breakfast.

I brought up an analogy of a plain salad and how tasteless it would be if we didn't add various items like we do at the salad bar. Compare this to what our economy would be like without our ethnic, minority and diverse entrepreneurs and the goods and services they provide.

Many times we recognize the corporate businesses and organizations on accepting diversity and do not always salute our minority small businesses and entrepreneurs who have overcome many barriers to entry into the marketplace.

During our last great economic recession, I was asked to speak at the state Hmong Business Convention. The topic they wanted to hear was, *Opportunities for Business Expansion and Growth.* This was true optimism in our free enterprise system.

Many see self-employment as better security than a wage job. They also realize it is a way for self-sufficiency for their family. They understand:

- Dedication to hard work
- Have an economic lifestyle
- Acceptance of risk
- Cultural social values and loyalty

The community must embrace them as connectors to help them be a part of economic gardening. Over the years we have seen them recognized as solid employers, investors and tax base to our community. These entrepreneurs understand the expression, "small boats rise on an incoming tide." Let's salute, embrace and support them.

"Success is not measured by what a man accomplishes, but by the opposition he has encountered and the courage with which he has maintained the struggle against overwhelming odds."

- Charles Lindbergh

CHAPTER 74

Defying Gravity: High Growth "Entronauts" in a Slow Economy

Being a high growth entrepreneur in a tough economy is not an easy journey. Even during an expanding economy there are many bumps along the way and challenges that hold many businesses down. Many are told it isn't possible to grow and the risk is too great. That's exactly what our space program and astronauts were told about landing on the moon.

I have had the privilege to teach, mentor and work with hundreds of these growth *entronauts*. These entrepreneurs have come from all walks of life, are highly diverse and are the hope and future for job and wealth creation.

"Entronauts continue to innovate, invest, persevere and grow during tough journeys. They are the ones who can see around the bend. They defy gravity."

We need to help support their visions, even if they start as micro-enterprises. They become our small giants and leaders. A lot of small businesses add up to a lot of jobs for our communities.

Some do not allow for failure but don't succeed. Others take the path to progress, to growth, and feel the freedom of enterprise. They conquer themselves and not just others.

Many ask where the new and growth businesses are coming from.

Here is a history of the profiles:

- Late 90's and early 2000's – Retail, coffee, restaurants, arts and photography

- Late 2000's – Business services such as graphic arts, web page, accounting, payroll and human resources

- 2010 – Wellness, health and fitness, GPS systems, video and eco-friendly products and services

- 2015– Innovative healthcare systems, organic and urban farming, and the resurgence of light manufacturing, including 3D printing

- 2018 – Digital and mobile technology, new learning systems, nutrition, water quality systems, apps and creative arts

CHAPTER 75

Motivating Entrepreneurs
Into Champions

As I drive through Wisconsin during one of the most beautiful times of the year, I see how blessed we are with the brilliance of fall colors in the landscape. As I listen to the sports networks, I am caught by the action of our exciting sports teams from the Wisconsin Badgers, the Green Bay Packers, as well as the Milwaukee Brewers.

As I speak to audiences in classes, book signings and workshops, I am energized by the entrepreneurs who are such positive individuals. It is a task at times to motivate during challenging economic times. This is showing entrepreneurs the right journey and motivating them for success. To be able to "wow" an audience is the magic of inspiration. You may be a good storyteller but talking about a tragedy or success is not always the answer.

There must be a learning awareness, enlightenment and a solution to create a teaching moment. Motivation for entrepreneurs can get complicated because of the risk, challenges, and commitment.

Let's talk about the motivation that drives sports stars and legends as well as entrepreneurial champions.

Material Things:
They stimulate our senses. Our modern society is full of entertainment, rewards, enticements, sports cars, exotic travel and retiring early. Where is your compass and journey taking you?

Contribution and Charitable Giving:
Causes that touch our heart along with the ability to give to people in need are crucial. Giving back is our social responsibility.

Familiarizing oneself with the needs of others is important so that we can serve the underserved. This can be done powerfully through entrepreneurship. Donations can leverage a lot if given as "heart power."

Recognition:
Leaders crave recognition and appreciation. They need a spirit of approval. Character must be earned.

Respect:
Do not worry about getting the approval of everyone. It is often out of your control and there will always be jealous and envious people. Seek respect from those who are successful and caring.

Purpose:
This is a strong motivator and is often the most satisfying for many. It is the needle that points north. These are true leaders. They do not determine their purpose, they sense it. Purpose takes them out of the realm of living only for themselves and material things. They explore a meaningful and happy live.

Destiny:
Destiny is the journey to success but also of fulfillment and motivation. Understanding your journey can be inspiring and keep your sustainability going. These are leaders who have built-in goals and give back their gift of talent.

Legacy:
We can all leave a footprint. Whether it was Reggie White or Steve Jobs, they have left us a legacy to remember. Contribute and feel good about our accomplishments after our death. Whether it is sports figures or entrepreneurial champions, we all have dreams. It is about what motivates us. Look for your reward in having achieving something for your community and not just money.

CHAPTER 76

Our True Heroes

The general public, not to mention the small businesses themselves, are getting mixed messages and questions are raised about who provides the funding for small micro-businesses?
- Where does the money come from for business start-ups?
- Who helps in financing the growth of small businesses?

It is ironic that on the front page of our recent local newspaper, leaders were speaking of stimulus money and loans that are flowing to small businesses, and on the next page is an article headline that reads: ***Small companies denied credit. Big business firms have more access to loans.*** Ben Bernanke, former Federal Reserve Chairman further stated, "Making credit accessible to sound small businesses is crucial to our economic recovery. More must be done."

The business question to note is, "Does our government really let the public know who provides the steam that drives the small business engine which drives our economy? You will be surprised to learn new ventures are funded 80% by owner and family savings and finances.

"What does this mean? Our true heroes for investing money back into our economy are our hard working citizens and their close friends and families who truly believe in our free enterprise system."

After going through four major recessions as an entrepreneur, owner and consultant, I feel that the financial lending playing field has changed. Entrepreneurs will see different investors in the future to support their business. They will continue to bootstrap and work hard. I see jobs created every week from entrepreneurs, which is a slow process but an encouraging sign, which we refer to as "Economic Gardening."

Entrepreneur programs continue our mission of economic gardening that includes planting the seeds, helping cultivate resources and utilizing the tools of other entrepreneurs to grow our economic landscape. But investors and financial organizations must also step up to the plate. Entrepreneurs are not looking for a handout, just some breaks that big businesses and other organizations receive, such as:

- The government started giving students, who had federal loan debts, who opt for public government jobs to walk away from their debt. Should not entrepreneurs who provide jobs have some forgiveness or breaks as well?

- Should not angel investors get more tax breaks on job creation?

- Local governments and businesses need to support and invest in entrepreneur programs, such as E-Hub which helps produce and retain entrepreneurs who provide taxes, jobs and goods and services to our community.

In conclusion, it is about access to capital but also creating a level playing field for entrepreneurs or they will fail to exist.

CHAPTER 77

The Missing Ingredient:
Finding the Money

In past meetings at the United States Treasury Department in downtown Chicago, I have had the opportunity to discuss the state of affairs for small business lending and serve as an advocate for under-served target markets for entrepreneurs.

I see it as a three-legged stool. Financial lenders and banks have the money, and entrepreneurs and micro enterprises need the money to launch innovative enterprises. The equation needs to be filled with the third leg of the stool. The missing ingredient. . . *technical assistance.*

You cannot just walk into a bank and throw an idea against the wall and expect the loan committee to accept it, especially in today's world.

Even worse, you cannot go to a small business support or non-profit organization and be looking for free money or grants that are not available. What are possibly available are loans with low interest rates if you fill some of the C's of credit (collateral, character, conditions, capacity, capital). Yes, there are angel investors, family and friends, and your savings, but you still need to convince them with a business plan, which is getting you "loan ready" or "investment ready."

Loans are big business for micro-business owners. Using all three sides of the three-legged stool, I want to help give you a perspective on how a well-prepared borrower can negotiate from a position of strength, saving you money, time and aggravation.

Before you put your hand out to begin borrowing, here are some things that will help:

- **Be Personal:** You must build a trust factor with your lender or investor. Invite them to your business, impress them with products or take them to a client who was impressed with your services. Ask the banker their expertise and other services.

- **Understand your business:** The phrase, "learn by your mistakes" should not be used. You need to be prudent and wise and take a class on understanding the elements that are needed in your entrepreneurial journey.

- **Finding good mentors and advisors.** You need to know how to form a solid **Enterprise Team**.

- **A solid business plan.** This means one that you helped format, not a template from the Internet or from the shelf at a library or bookstore.

- The vision, mission and value statements must come from you. The lender is looking for **character and not characters.**

- **Technical expertise,** market intelligence, financial assumptions and cash flow projections. You need professional expertise.

- **Put together an entrepreneurial profile.** This can be learned!
  - o Entrepreneurial small business classes help mold your journey.
  - o Management and technical training in your field.
  - o Sometimes this may be a certification in your field.
  - o Listing your strengths and past expertise is very important.
  - o Surround your business with solid employees.

- **Your budget** must not be overly optimistic. You need to have a back-up plan and in some cases an exit strategy.

- **Plan not to fail.** Write down some challenges that may occur and how you will overcome them. You cannot ignore some of the failures that may occur. You need to show the bank how you are helping them reduce its exposure to risk.

- **Put some of your skin in the game.** Yes, this is collateral. It may be savings in some form, real estate or equipment, or notes payable from investors or friends.

- **Understand gap financing.** Sometimes a micro-lender or some other creative financing can be used. A professional can help put this together.

Be prepared. Listen to advice. Be patient. Understand your market. Put together a solid business plan and enterprise team.

Now you are ready to put your hand out.

"What we really want to do is what we are really meant to do. When we do what we are meant to do, money comes to us, doors open for us, we feel useful, and the work we do feels like play to us."

- Julia Cameron

"People are like storage batteries, constantly discharging energy. They must be recharged or they will run low. Recognition is the art of recharging people who have gone the extra mile. It is truly a gift worth giving. Create moments to remember."

CHAPTER 78

Is Franchising For You?

Having a secure job in the private corporate business world for 25-35 years is just not a reality anymore. Todays ever-changing economy is forcing people to embark on new paths because of being downsized or retiring early or not having a chance to enter the job pool.

I talk to several clients each year, evaluating the possibility of buying a franchise as the path to entrepreneurship. I normally do an industry market analysis to check the feasibility, and then they enroll in entrepreneur classes and prepare a business plan. I advise them to establish an enterprise team and then determine the advantages and disadvantages to pursue in the endeavor.

The next several years will be growth years for franchises according to the SBA and their organization.

Some of the advantages for franchises:
- You have a turnkey proven business model.
- You receive on-going training and support.
- Access to new products, equipment and technology.

Some of the disadvantages:
- It is not a guarantee for success. It still has risks like any other business.
- It is a longer-term commitment.
- There may be strings attached.

Part of the journey is the selection of a franchise:
- Conduct market research.
- Carefully look at the image and strength of the franchise.
- Evaluate competition. Do not get passionate about a short-term fad, which tends to draw a lot of competitors.

- Have an attorney go over the Franchise Disclosure Document. This provides the detail in your contract agreements.
- Take an entrepreneur course.
- Build your professional enterprise team.
- Set aside money to pay for start-up fees and start-up costs.

"Your work is going to fill a large part of your life, and the only way to be truly satisfied is to do what you believe is great work.
And the only way to do great work is to love what you do."

- Steve Jobs

CHAPTER 79

Amp up Your Presentation Style?

I was recently asked if entrepreneurs needed to be good speakers. Are we really delivering the message we intend with our presentations? There are various forms of presentations and they all serve different purposes.

Today we are in a PowerPoint world. Many presentations are given every day using PowerPoint; however, they are very slow, non-creative, and dull. From the many conferences and talks I have witnessed each year, the audience just wants copies of the slides so they can leave the room. Audiences are used to *"Death by PowerPoint"* and many of us just go along with it.

Video is a tool to incorporate into PowerPoint to bring it to a new level. In general, the use of PowerPoint for inspiring presentations has been a disaster.

When coaching my mentors, coaches, consultants and entrepreneurs, I recommend presentations that will master design, tell stories, share a meaning and have emotion.

Having the opportunity to speak nationally and internationally, I suggest ditching PowerPoint and giving a handout with bullet points at the end of the presentation. Use emotion and meaning during the talk and presentation.

Use PowerPoint only as a document tool. Designing powerful visuals is exciting unless it gets to become an old-fashioned slide presentation where you lose your audience.

Get out of your comfort zone of PowerPoint. Challenge yourself to develop your creativity and transform your speaking and presentation efforts.
Your presentation is like the tie or clothes you wear. It tells your audience a lot about you.

Here are just a few tips that I hope will be of benefit to you.
- Don't hold back. If you have a reason for your topic, let people know it.
- You need to notice if your audience is **with you**.
- Preparation is not overrated.
- Even if you are well prepared be totally aware, remain flexible to the moment and to anything that arises.
- Be yourself and speak from the heart.
- Never apologize at first for something.
- Do homework on your audience.
- A presentation is a journey with a purpose. Don't start out unless you know your destination.
- Lastly, enjoy it. When you do, chances are the audience will as well.

You can judge how your connection with the audience is going by seeing smiles, heads nodding in agreement and feet tapping. This connection will give you a great feeling and inspire you to do more presentations.

When asking instructors or trainers to provide a consistent means of presentation, the PowerPoint method works well as long as the instructor or trainer engages the audience and relays many real life situations and stories. They should hold off on the hand out until after the presentation, unless it is in a workbook.

Presentation importance:
- Your speaking ability will evolve you as a leader.
- Your pitch will help you get investors.
- Your negotiating skills will win you contracts. Your business modeling and storytelling will help you shape your vision and mission to recruit good people.
- Your business plan presentation will help you find the money.

CHAPTER 80

Entrepreneurs Evolve as Leaders

One of the amazing things about entrepreneurship is the power of unique ideas. Many of our businesses have evolved as champions. As leaders we need to nurture our creative imaginations. New ideas rock the boat and cost money. Money is only one aspect. We also need energy. Energy is another needed ingredient as a leader. Many have come through our program to reboot their business. They learn about empowerment.

Empowerment plugs the leaks. Our challenges are toxic people, bad habits, fear and indecision. Leaders fill their tank with faith, hope, prayers and laughter. Leaders have an attitude of perseverance.

As graduates you have learned to develop and reinforce solid business ethics and core values. Leaders seek counsel to learn. Peer-to-peer mentorship is important.

Some of your team will embrace your vision and others will not. Next you need to cultivate as leaders your need to pull the weeds. Negativity is toxic.

You have learned that customer fulfillment must be nourished as the lifeblood of your business. Entrepreneurs evolve as leaders when they develop the heart to serve.

Some final thoughts:
- Don't be fearful of hard work or the challenges during your entrepreneurial journey.
- Believe in your dreams!
- Be proud of your entrepreneurial contributions.
- As leaders you need to continue to grow. You will evolve as leaders by building a strong community.

"As a leader, you must never ever underestimate the power of hope. Without it you will fail. Optimism is the faith that leads to achievement. Nothing can be done without hope. It's true we live as entrepreneurs in a negative world, but we must reinforce it with the positive."

CHAPTER 81

A Dose of Reality

In my book, *The Evolutionally Entrepreneur…Going Beyond the Passion,* I emphasize that passion is the motor that drives the entrepreneur; but it can also become your worst enemy! When Tina Dettman-Bielefeldt, the Regional Director of SCORE, asked me about business failures, I mentioned that entrepreneurs live on the edge of risk most of the time.

Successful entrepreneurs know how to handle challenges, yet many have blinders on from their own passion. New business failure, many times, is due to the lack of objectivity. Tina has interviewed many of our alumni entrepreneurs for her weekly SCORE column in the Green Bay Press Gazette.

E-Hub's signature series, "Stepping Up to New Opportunities" lets potential entrepreneurs recognize the journey and challenges in the true sense that *you cannot always afford to learn from your mistakes.* The series offers a snapshot of detours and dangers – signs to watch for. The dose of reality is not to just grow your business, but to parent it.

There are hundreds of books and articles on successful entrepreneurs. To achieve success, we teach entrepreneurs how to avoid failure. In our *Mentor Advantage* series, we show mentors, business advisors and counselors how they must learn to clear the terrain of failure factors.

The business plan and business experience itself does not guarantee success. The mistakes usually come from the same drive that got the entrepreneur there to begin with – *passion.*

Businesses do not always fail due to the lack of technical expertise. Other factors include:
- Health or health insurance
- Lack of common sense

- Misplaced fears
- Believing success is totally reliant on the idea
- Not understanding family needs and the balance of life
- Not knowing how/when to shed unprofitable products and services or how to exit into another sector of business
- Giving equal reward for unequal contributions for employees or partners.

Being an entrepreneur is a large dose of reality. It is looking at life which others may deem uncomfortable. True entrepreneurs get a certain amount of pleasure with this uncertainty.

Always keep in mind: Failure is not losing. It is having been given an opportunity in the first place. However, the *dose of reality* is preparation and understanding going along with the passion.

"Make the most of yourself by fanning the tiny, inner sparks of possibility into flames of achievement."

- Golda Meir

CHAPTER 82

Business Modeling:
The New Rules of the Game

Why Business Modeling?
We cannot adapt quickly enough with just business plans to survive the accelerating rate of changes in the marketplace.

The New Rules of the Game:

1. Customer: The customers have changed and they are better informed. They want fast service! They want transparency.

2. The Internet: It serves as a platform to launch a new business. It helps us connect, shop, entertain and communicate 24/7/365.

3. Social Value: Is here to stay – it's a way to distinguish yourself from the competition.

4. Technology: Is changing every second and is widely available. It is cheap. We can use technology at no cost such as Skype, Word Press and more.

5. Hitting the bull's eye in relevance to your target customer is your winning game plan. We are overloaded with information. Just-in-time delivery makes our buying decisions easier. Learning to design, mobilize and implement your business model and then manage, adapt and respond to this new economy will help you to succeed as an entrepreneur.

Business Model Defined:
A business model is an explanation of the way a business creates value for customers, how value is delivered to customers and how the company captures profits.

183

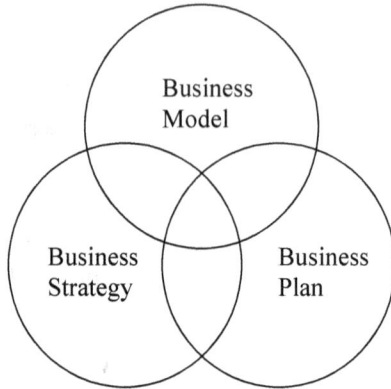

Evolutions Business Group Model

Business Model Evolution:
Building a core business is essential, but after reviewing your basic business model you must reinvent and evolve your current business model. This will provide for higher growth, but also give you protection against other innovative competitive companies. You need to develop a long-term business strategy for a new-niche-central business model that has an impact on performance.

Evolutionary barriers:
The first is shifting of assets that are needed due to operational or marketing expenses. The second is cognitive - the inability of owners, managers and staff to change to the current business models.

How do you overcome these barriers?
Construct maps of business models. The new evolutionary process is a discovery driven process of experimentation. This planning helps you create a culture that encourages employees to the objectives "what if." The core element and logic of the business model revolves around the firm revenues and costs, its value proposition to the customers and the avenue to capture that

value. In the end, the business model can serve as a vehicle for innovation as well as a source of innovation.

As markets develop, companies compete by focusing on adding:
- Features
- Reliability
- Convenience
- Speed
- Commodity on price

The implementation of a new business model delivers a more compelling customer value proposition thus growing revenue and profits. The most important aspect and focal point of designing your business model is the **Value Proposition**, which I explain in an earlier chapter.

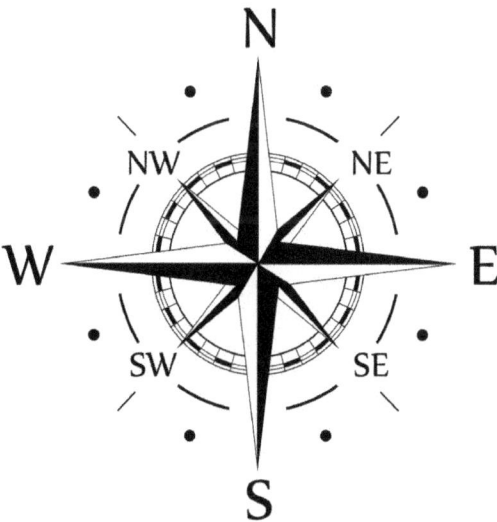

"Successful people do what unsuccessful people are not willing to do. Don't wish it were easier; wish you were better."

- Jim Rohn

CHAPTER 83

Don't Build Your Own Cage

There are many challenges in today's entrepreneurial workplace including change, competition, deadlines and understaffing.

Employees and owners/managers alike may feel under pressure at times. Some pressure may help us reach our goals but too much pressure can adversely affect our health, well-being and productivity. This includes the entrepreneurs and their staffs.

Here are some of my tips to help manage work-related pressure:

- Sometimes we work our "super producer" to the point of burning them out. Be aware of your employee's workloads.

- Make sure that work is appropriately distributed. Some people never say no even when they are overloaded.

- Work with people to help them prioritize tasks. Coach them to manage demands to reduce stress from customers and clients.

- Employees must negotiate for resources when certain projects get them overwhelmed.

- I have found that communicating with employees as a mentor and not as a boss is a payback in moral and will outweigh the cost of the time you spend.

- Coach them to have a sense of control. Encourage them to take baby steps to get things done. Work at building trust. Be open and honest. Build a trustworthy relationship.

- Organize and provide a training program that works on technical and customer service to handle challenging days.

- Share the vision and mission especially during tough times.

- Encourage staffs to be emotionally and physically fit. Stress the importance of health and a good life balance with friends and family.

- Share your knowledge.

- Be available for questions or concerns.

- Finally, give recognition. People need to feel appreciated. I would often send a letter home to their family.

Someone once asked me, "Why would we train people when they sometimes leave?" I responded with, "Where would we be at if we didn't train people?"

Now for yourself:
- Tame your inbox.
- Stop allowing e-mail to dominate your life.
  It interrupts your concentration.
  It puts you in a constant state of anticipation.
  Break the cycle...disconnect!
- Give yourself time to think.
- Now is the time to choose freedom.

Too often we make our own cages of our mind or the heart. We allow technology to make them for us. Go on a data diet – only consume gourmet data. Data is only information, not wisdom, foresight or knowledge. We have the keys to unlock them.

Unlock your stress today...make entrepreneurship a freedom.

CHAPTER 84

Embark on Innovation
for Your Treasure Hunt

During the journey working as a CEO and owner of companies which had steady growth and also as a business architect helping entrepreneurs grow their business, adherence was needed while on the path.

In most cases everyone is looking for a secret treasure chest. In a treasure hunt you need a map but also some innovative thinkers to beat the competition to the hidden treasure.

With this thought in mind, you need to change your approach, culture and innovation. The difficulty of innovation is in the communication to pursue the change.

Smaller companies can adapt and change faster than larger companies and competitors. But do they? No, because change can be difficult and there are more risks involved. I consider it a risk *not to be innovative!*

Owners and management look at change as messy. They don't want to embark on change or the treasure hunt. Yes, change does keep things in a flux. Some entrepreneurs say they want to be innovative but end up being late adopters and follow.

Is Innovation Obtainable?

Innovative skills can be taught and learned. A good leader, mentor or coach can guide an organization through the process.

Visionary leaders are not afraid of reaching out for the hunt. Their passion has no barriers, but they need to inspire the trust and confidence with the rest of their organization and their customers.

This can be done with a good balance to maintain productivity in today's operations to keep the cash flow and profits going…but also to maintain an eye for the future.

Innovation needs different types of resources. Smaller companies can adapt and change faster than larger companies and competitors. But do they?

I like to use the word "co-creation" instead of collaboration. This opens the door to partnering with others to open up your playing field to change.

One internal innovative tool I find that works for staffs to improve themselves is to have them pay for their own training. Yes, they pay for the investment because it gets them more engaged. Instead of paying for their future assets and walking out the door, you pay them bonuses or payroll increases based on their takeaway from the seminar or conference. They will engage more and are more productive in achieving your goals as well as theirs.

Entrepreneurs cannot be afraid of disruptive change. Remember, the butterfly goes through a tremendous transformation before starting its journey.

"Chase the vision, not the money, the money will end up following you."

- Tony Hsieh

CHAPTER 85

A Positive Look for the Future of Entrepreneurs

As I see each decade fly by, **_shift happens_**. One of the yearly themes for E-Hub businesses was "Evolve...Reinvent Yourself."

Many entrepreneurs have used true innovation to advance or expand their businesses. If we were to predict 2025, what would the crystal ball tell us?

> • Where will our customers come from?
> • What about our careers and job growth?
> • What about the industries in the marketplace?

Some major hurdles to consider will be the speed of change, higher risks, lifestyles, immigration, technology, and aging population.

These are a few predictions I'd like to make for the future:

- Innovation will be a key to entrepreneurship, democracy, education, and America's strength in the world marketplace.
- Immigration will be a major part of jobs, healthcare and security.
- More use of DNA and genetics for healthcare and longevity.
- Innovative fitness programs to adapt to many lifestyles.
- A strong wireless network nation will advance entirely new business strategies.
- The lack of future readiness of U.S. workforce will change into better skills.
- Energy costs will play a significant factor in the way we estimate our expenses.

- Privatization in the government sector will be an opportunity for many.
- Personal and internet security will be a major factor.
- More countries will have democracy and western culture demands.
- The future of entertainment from music, movies and television will change dramatically.
- There will be more jobs in math, science and technology than people to fill them.
- Meeting the challenges of the baby boomers and multicultural population will redefine our new marketplace.

"Young entrepreneurs are our gift for the future. They have the unique capacity to be innovative, persevere, adapt to changes and seize new opportunities, thus being the most powerful forces that will shape our future."

CHAPTER 86

Detours are Part of the Journey

When you launch your entrepreneurial journey you will not always know what bumps, potholes and obstacles will set you on to different paths.

Challenges signal for you to evolve and change directions...many times taking a detour.

The question I like to ask is how an entrepreneur handles them? This journey is one way. No matter how many detours you take, none can take you back.

The key is to keep striving to move forward making the best of the journey and turning the challenges into positives.

Watch out for the blind spots! Fear of the unknown is part of life. Most of the time we cannot control circumstances, but we cannot stop in the middle of the road either. We must move on.

I am asked dozens of times about the crystal ball and if a certain business will be successful. First of all, you need the vision and dream. Next you need the pillars of running a business; the work experience, the enterprise team and preparation.

Along the way you may fall down, but understand that these failures make you stronger.

If you are lost find your compass. . . your mentor. They are gifts in your journey. They see your road as a path to possibility. Some just warm your heart with support.

193

"Vision is the art of seeing what is invisible to others. Our vision and passion must be applied. It is not just starting a race, but being able to visualize it and knowing instinctively how to win it. The same concept holds true for evolutionary entrepreneurs."

CHAPTER 87

Evolving into an Entrepreneur of Influence

Many people I meet who are in business or want to start a business feel they want to make a difference in today's world. Sometimes they are already retired from their career but feel they want to make a difference as a mentor or giving back in some way.

To make a difference is becoming a person of influence. You must do what you love doing. People need to see the passion inside of you shining through. Some people have been productive but don't feel they have made a difference or been a person of influence.

Productive people become insecure or worried someone may take their job, so they work through vacations and stay away from the balance of life they need.

These people have gone through life with an environment of the bar not being raised. They've operated under the status quo and learned not to rock the boat.

Here's a question for you . . .Do you want to be shown the path? Or, do you want to create one?

The traditional career path is over. My grandfather and father had long-term careers. I grew up in a blue-collar family environment. My career path after college started as an executive in a fast growing regional department store in operations and logistics.

To make a difference, my passion carried me into entrepreneurship. Growing a couple of small businesses into multi-million dollar businesses opened the door to building several communities by giving back, serving on Chamber boards, non-profits and civic organizations.

To raise the bar in making a difference as an entrepreneur of influence, you should consider they key strengths to set yourself apart:

- Raise your image via your brand. Your profile needs to stand out.
- You need to establish great connections. To make the connections, you must raise your value to establish these partnerships.
- Package your skills and talents and turn them into products or services to become profitable.
- Build an amazing pitch to set yourself apart.
- Write and publish your concepts and ideas. Writing blogs, guest columns or books can do this.
- Design and build a blueprint for your business model.

"When roadblocks, locked gates and unexpected turns sprout up along our paths, we map things out or we quit on the spot and progress no further. Or, we can build a new path and follow it in whatever direction our imagination takes us. For those who dream, the choice is simple."

- James Merrell

CHAPTER 88

Engage - Put the Icing on the Cake

When speaking to the many entrepreneurs, I enjoy spending time helping them find their entrepreneurial assets, market analysis, competitive strategies and much more.

It not only goes beyond your passion, academic intelligence or even entrepreneurial spirit, but the ability to connect or as I call it cupiding© thus *putting the icing on the cake.*

Unfortunately, I have seen these connections lost in a fraction of the amount of time in which it took to develop them. It ends up back to the "me, me, me" attitude. True engaging needs to be made with feeling, purpose and honesty.

To the many new entrepreneurs: It is not the mountain you conquer, but yourself. Career and life success happens from "engaging."
It is the ability to overcome obstacles.

Nobody can go along their journey by starting a new beginning, but anyone can start today and take a new path. We are seeing many people who have lost their jobs, become burned out in their careers, or who have hit the bottom.

To become successful they must learn to engage in a new or specialized skill. They have to fight off the *crisis* status and turn to the *opportunity* status. For many of you, I push you to the unsettling; it is pushing you out of the nest to take freedom of flight. That is what I am always hoping for in the end.

Many new entrepreneurs come with super burn out which afflicts successful people who find their careers are no longer rewarding. They need to be engaged as well if they want to make a difference. They need to get involved in the sense of giving

197

back. Opening up a micro enterprise that leads to social responsibility is that solution.

It is the *icing on the cake* in their life.

They must remember that even on the cloudiest days the sun is still there, just behind the clouds waiting to shine.

I applaud many of you for *reclaiming the fire.*

We also applaud you as entrepreneurs for not just waiting for luck or the goose who laid the golden egg, but to the ones who are making the opportunities happen.

You will become the makers not the takers.

Many of the entrepreneurs who went through our programs have become award winners, community leaders, mentors, and champion entrepreneurs. They all have been a part of increasing the quality of life in our communities. This is one of the most important ingredients in retention and sustainability in building a creative and innovative community. They have become *engaged.*

Many of you reading this book will become investors, entrepreneurs, civic leaders and creators. You will all become spokes in the wheel that are connected to a hub that makes the economy roll.

By engaging with others, you will become pillars in your community . . . and yes, *you will become small giants!*

The Butterfly Effect:
Making a Difference

I want to end this book by showing you how the butterfly effect works in the entrepreneurial world. The once legendary "Butterfly Effect," coined by a scientist almost 50 years ago has become the basis for a branch of mathematics known as *chaos theory*, which has been applied in countless scenarios since its introduction.

The butterfly effect is a metaphor for the concept that small, seemingly insignificant events like the fluttering of a butterfly's wings can produce tremendous and unanticipated consequences.

So what's my point? Every entrepreneur or dreamer has been created to make a difference. Your life matters, your ideas have value, and your actions have meaning as you embark on your new path!

Mark Burwell

About the author

As a compelling author and speaker, Mark Burwell informs, challenges, inspires and leaves you with a new and powerful understanding of your business, community, customers, staff and lives. As a successful serial entrepreneur, mentor, business architect, columnist, non-profit and senior executive, he draws on over 35 years of working with more than 3,000 entrepreneurs.

As CEO of a Midwest based menswear apparel firm, he grew the business into a nationally recognized retail, catalog and internet business.

He was honored as *Wisconsin's Small Business Advocate of the Year* by the U.S. Small Business Administration for creating a level playing field for small businesses. University of Wisconsin Stout awarded him the *Distinguished Alumni Award* of the year for his career, business and civic achievements. He received a Bachelor's Degree in Business Administration and Public Address while becoming a collegiate All-American in track. The University recently inducted him into the College of Management Cabot Executive In Residence Wall of Honor.

Mark received the *2008 Innovation Champions' Award* at the annual Ideas to Profits Conference. The award was presented for his work in advancing innovative entrepreneurship in Wisconsin and the positive community effect it has had.

Mark has served on numerous business chambers, business advisory boards, and civic groups as chairman and president, as well as statewide boards and advisory panels. As president and owner of Evolutions Business Group, he has studied, lectured and consulted nationally as well as internationally.

Mark has also been engaged with the New North, a collaborative economic development initiative as past chair of the entrepreneurial committee and Fast Forward Mentorship program. He has led classes and workshops as adjunct faculty at several colleges, currently at the Venture Center – Fox Valley Technical College.

Mark is the Director Emeritus for the Urban Hope Entrepreneur Center, known as "E-Hub" (Entrepreneur Hub) whereby he has been the architect for the successful model and concepts in practice.

www.ingramcontent.com/pod-product-compliance
Lightning Source LLC
Chambersburg PA
CBHW060300220326
41598CB00027B/4183